I0479023

A Primer

—on—

Theatre and Aesthetics

A Primer

—on—

Theatre and Aesthetics

Performance and Social Change

LAUREN D. FRIESEN

Foreword by Elizabeth Kattner

PICKWICK *Publications* • Eugene, Oregon

A PRIMER ON THEATRE AND AESTHETICS
Performance and Social Change

Pickwick Publications
An Imprint of Wipf and Stock Publishers
199 W. 8th Ave., Suite 3
Eugene, OR 97401

www.wipfandstock.com

PAPERBACK ISBN: 979-8-3852-1432-7
HARDCOVER ISBN: 979-8-3852-1433-4
EBOOK ISBN: 979-8-3852-1434-1

Cataloguing-in-Publication data:

Names: Friesen, Lauren D. [author]. | Kattner, Elizabeth [foreword writer].

Title: A primer on theatre and aesthetics : performance and social change / by Lauren D. Friesen.

Description: Eugene, OR: Pickwick Publications, 2024 | Includes bibliographical references and index.

Identifiers: ISBN 979-8-3852-1432-7 (paperback) | ISBN 979-8-3852-1433-4 (hardcover) | ISBN 979-8-3852-1434-1 (ebook)

Subjects: LCSH: Theater and philosophy. | Theater—Philosophy. | Drama—History and criticism—Theory, etc. | Aesthetics. | Art—Philosophy.

Classification: PN2039 F75 2024 (paperback) | PN2039 (ebook)

VERSION NUMBER 072924

Cover Art: "Transitions"—a monotype print by Janet Friesen

With gratitude to my former professors and the students in my aesthetics and theatre history courses.

Dedicated to Janet, Erica, Bayrex, Eliot, Carrie, August, Max, Greta, and Alexandra

"In a world of lies and liars, an honest work of art
is always an act of social responsibility."[1]

—Robert McKee

1. Robert McKee, *Story: Substance, Structure, Style, and the Principles of Screenwriting* (Los Angeles: ReganBooks, 1997).

Contents

Acknowledgments

There are many individuals who need to be recognized because they played a pivotal role in the development of this book. Students at Goshen College and the University of Michigan examined these issues with considerable diligence. In addition, I presented papers at conferences in the United States, Canada, Germany, and Great Britain. Feedback from peers in those settings provided numerous suggestions for continued research.

I thank my professors at Bethel College in Kansas, the Anabaptist Mennonite Biblical Seminary in Indiana, the Pacific School of Religion, the Graduate Theological Union, and the University of California, Berkeley. The guidance of the people who diligently taught in the fields of history, theatre, theology, and philosophy provided a foundation for my own research. My deepest gratitude goes to professors Keith Sprunger, C. J. Dyck, Leland Harder, William Gering, Delbert Wiens, Mia Mochizuki, Douglas Adams, Wayne Rood, Margaret Wilkerson, Dunbar Ogden III, and Marvin Rosenberg. Without their encouragement and diligence, my path would have followed the road many have traveled. Obviously, I took the other one.

I chaired the Theatre and Religion section for the Association in Higher Education for six years. Several publications, *Theatre and Religion I, II,* and *III,* emerged from those symposia and received wide circulation.

Professor Horst Schwebel at Philipps-Universität Marburg and Klaus Hoffmann with the German Federal Division of

Education and the Arts invited me to present papers on theatre and religion at numerous conferences and symposiums. Their institutions modeled how the arts are vital for investigating intersections between culture, religion, and philosophy. Their encouragement and feedback have been influential.

I was a member of the Kennedy Center's National Playwriting Program and served three years as chair. In that capacity, I read many new scripts, attended theatre festivals across the nation, and visited many campuses as a production respondent. In that capacity, I saw the vital role that theatre has in academia and society. Those were exhilarating years.

This volume is based on my final lectures on aesthetics and theatre at the Horace Rackham School of Graduate Studies at the University of Michigan. The class was always a delight—because the graduate students were so deeply engaged in the issues discussed in these pages.

As will become clear, without Plato and Aristotle, the ideas in this brief study might not have existed. A round of applause for the ancient Greeks and their courage and insight. As one of my professors once stated, "we may be mere footnotes to their dispute!"

I tend to favor the term "aesthetics" and seldom use the phrase "philosophy of art," although these words speak to the same field of inquiry. Along with the term aesthetics, it is important to recognize that its opposite is anesthetic! The opposite of art is numbness, even induced sleep. Aesthetics implies sensation, awareness, movement, and consciousness.

I will always owe a deep sense of gratitude to my wife Janet and her support for my work and to my children and grandchildren, who always provide a lot of joy.

As you read this, somewhere on the globe, a stage manager is calling out, "Places, lights, action!"

Foreword

What does real, tangible, practical art—a play, a ballet, or a sculpture—have to do with philosophy and textual scholarship? Is not art meant to be experienced and does not the act of writing about it and relegating it to the pages of a book kill its life? These questions were at the forefront of my mind as I made the transition from a practicing dance artist who created movement to a dance scholar who wrote about it. It was my privilege to have Dr. Lauren Friesen as department chair in my first teaching position a few months after defending my dissertation, and he mentored my first postgraduate school endeavors to write and organize two quite different processes into coherent work. I learned from him that these are not separate practices, but that aesthetics and artistic product serve one another and, since that time, it has been my endeavor to continue to draw connections between them. I was honored to be asked to write a short preface to this volume, which is truly a gem, outlining millennia of complex ideas in a way that allows the reader to make connections across the years and art genres. Questions I have been pondering since I committed myself at a young age to the art of dance became clear to me and enabled a deeper understanding of works I have performed, taught, and taught about.

This book provides the reader an overview of many of the most important Western writings about art and beauty, contextualizing them with today's global art movements. In our digital age, artificial intelligence is only the latest technology to impact our understanding of what it means to create. The way art is transmitted to the masses continues to change at a neck breaking speed, making the need for considering it alongside tradition all the more important. In some academic settings, the study of the classics is somewhat frowned upon, deemed a relic of academia's Eurocentric past. There is certainly merit to this criticism. This book shows us the reason the field still matters, perhaps even more so as we deconstruct our past sins and failings as a society and look toward creating a more just world. Our ideas, thoughts, biases—both conscious and unconscious—were not developed in a void. We are shown how ideas of beauty and the arts are connected to generations of tradition, forming the foundation of how we perceive the world we live in, allowing us a richer experience of art as well as a deeper appreciation of it.

I have observed this phenomenon in the dance history classroom. Students are familiar with Michael Jackson's innovative "moon walk," which stunned and thrilled audiences when he first performed it in 1983. Most recognize how transformative his work was, but often unconsciously hold onto the myth of the creative genius who somehow mystically pulls ideas out of the ethers. In this case, Jackson's technique is based on centuries of African American dance tradition. Upon learning about the history and seeing films of the dancers that preceded him, students' appreciation for his dance does not lessen; in fact, it increases. They understand his work as a culmination of centuries of embodied art that spans continents. His genius lay in how he made it his own and then made it relevant for a new generation. His work endures decades later because he is part of a greater tradition.

This book creates a pathway for understanding aesthetic thought, a clear explanation of "how we got here." It rightly acknowledges that each of the philosophers discussed had personal failings, and their ideas were colored with the biases of the times they lived in, including those that perpetrated injustice. Some had their works misused as propaganda to justify atrocity. Many scholars have addressed these weaknesses. Other scholars address the exclusion of non-Western thought from our discourse, another important aspect of our growing body of knowledge. This book is not intended to address these issues directly; it was written to help us to understand what thinkers such as Aristotle, Immanuel Kant, and Friedrich Nietzsche have written, the positive aspects of their work that have endured, and how each of them has built upon the tradition of others. We are shown the importance of their work. We are constructing our knowledge of the world of art—music, dance, theatre, and visual arts—with the world we live in.

While reading the first few chapters of this book, I was struck with how clearly the connections are and, in some ways, the philosophical lineage, is laid out. I saw many things in a new light. My own evaluation of José Limón's dance *The Moor's Pavane* deepened as I reconsidered Limón's vision of the fate of a man of color by exploring it as part of the tradition promoting social justice. It is part of the lineage of artists from Aeschylus to William Shakespeare to Lin-Manuel Miranda. These artists have presented us with the world's injustices, and, at times, offer us solutions. Even more, this tradition is not just a Western one, and we are invited to ponder how traditions from around the globe are at once different and the same. This is evident as we consider the work of artists such as Chinese artist and activist Ai WeiWei.

Like Jackson, Miranda, and WeiWei have honed their natural talent with years of training and practice. To a certain extent, their work is notable in that it is part of a greater whole. Being part of this whole is also what can make a work timeless. An analysis such as presented in this book is not a requirement for knowing that a work is great, or for having an emotional experience, good or bad, to that work. Many people who enjoy art do not know its context in history, but even so they are moved by it. And for many, being moved is the important part and the work's *raison d'être*. But for those who create those works, including students who are themselves learning to be artists, the context and basis that aesthetics and this tradition can provide is essential. Even artists like Martha Graham, who considered her technique to be a sort of rebellion again classical dance, drew on themes from Greek mythology as well as choreographic conventions borrowed from the chorus in Greek theatre.

This volume ends with a discussion on social justice, demonstrating how theatre can expose injustice and promote progress. It shows the reader how we got here. We learned how Georg Hegel's notion of the power of art to bend history towards justice became the inspiration for Martin Luther King Jr.'s oft repeated: "the arc of the moral universe is long, but it bends toward justice." By examining our current progress in this context, we see that the pendulum swings of ideas may not be drastic as they seem, and we are, or we hope we are, moving in a positive direction.

In the final section, we are brought solidly into the theatre of today: What resonates with this generation? It is framed in the context of Arthur Danto's end of art—not the death of art—as the end of previous notions of tradition. Once again, we see why the study of aesthetics gives us a lens to first experience, and then to evaluate contemporary works. Importantly, we see how centuries of Western ideas of beauty, expression, and creativity can aid us as we encounter art from other parts of the world. We do not need to compare works or use our own values to judge art from various global traditions. We construct understanding from what we experience in our immediate environment, and we can use these impressions to gain a richer comprehension of why some things appeal to us and others do not.

In sum, the reader will find an overview of the work of some of the most important thinkers in the field of aesthetics, showing the best of what they wrote about the questions of their times and how they apply to contemporary art. Beginning in ancient Greece and by examining the foundational work of Plato and Aristotle, the reader is brought through the Dark Ages to the Enlightenment and shown how Augustine and Aquinas brought Greek philosophy directly into Medieval Catholic thought. These traditions have persisted for centuries in Western perceptions of beauty, brought forward by Kant, Hegel, and Nietzsche. The second chapter explores the work of important twentieth-century philosophers like Langer, Dewey, and Adams. Heidegger's complicated history is addressed, and the reader is invited to look at his work through the lens of centuries of philosophy, considering what is useful in his body work, not discounting it wholesale because of his connection to National Socialism, but also not forgetting the context in which he worked or excusing his shortcomings.

The final chapter pivots and shows how the rich history of aesthetics applies to theatre and art today, and we are shown how some of the most popular productions of the twenty-first century still contain echoes of the ancients. The purpose of art goes beyond experience and even catharsis. It is a vehicle that theatre in particular has provided for progress and social justice. In the sixteenth century, *Othello* laid bare white supremacy long before that term existed. In our generation, *Hamilton* sends a clear message that the injustices of revolutionary America still haunt us. As today's artists build new traditions on the foundation of what came before, this study shows that the arts continue to be a means by which the world can become a more just place.

Elizabeth Kattner
Professor of Dance
Oakland University

Introduction

There are many issues that arise when we discuss art and a record of that dialogue goes back 2,400 years. Basic questions include what art is, why it exists, and why there are artists. Why do people create art? Do you know art when you see it? Do you respond with delight, awe, agitation, or dislike? This brief introduction explores those issues.

We will also examine how people evaluate art. Can you tell the difference between a good work of art and one that lacks value? Must art have value to be considered worthwhile? If so, who can judge whether a work is any good? What happens in our thinking when we do not see any value in a work that is called art? Do such works also create an emotional response in us? What do we discover about ourselves when we explore artistic expression? And finally, does art have social value?

Is a sense of beauty innate in some people or learned? If it is learned, how does that happen? Is there a cause or reason why we have a sense of beauty? What value is it? Should religion be beautiful, or is beauty limited to things other than religious truths? This short volume mayn't answer all of these and many other questions, but it might begin dialogues on the arts.

What is the connection between feelings, thoughts, and actions? In other words, do the arts affect not just our emotions but also our behavior? How do the arts integrate those elements—or do they? Be on the lookout for clues. We will examine whether art unites or divides societies and nations. Can subcultures have meaningful art that is not part of the mainstream? Does art cause disruption or healing for a society? Can a work of art do both at the same time?

This study engages major philosophers who have given significant attention to the problems of aesthetics. My approach is to present the best of their point of view and allow the reader to weigh the merits of each one. Therefore, there are no "take-downs" in this brief volume. A second section examines plays by means of foregrounding their thematic content. This approach identifies themes in the plays and, from there, suggests how plot, character, and language can be understood and examined in greater depth. The brevity of this work means it is more illustrative than encyclopedic. It does not cover the multitudes of texts, topics, or voices that would be included in a much longer work.

The philosophers in this volume all formulated a philosophy of art. They addressed concerns and ideas that arose in their contexts and contributed to the Western tradition, which stretches from the classical Greeks until our time. The contributions they have made also speak to its limitations: Western writers often assume the superiority of Western methodology and ideas and, therefore, fail to investigate Asian, African, and Latin American aesthetics. In the coming years, these limitations may stimulate global research. The contribution of knowledge of the Western tradition will prepare readers to be informed about other traditions.

This volume presents a positive perspective on each philosopher rather than a deconstruction of their ideas or methods. Yet, the limitations of each method can be identified. Plato's views blend well with the perspectives of a monarchy. Aristotle's empiricism was also rooted in the Greek sense of superiority. Augustine accepted Plato's view on the need for a monarchy to rule with a sword and a bishop to guide the spirit. Yet, for all of Kant and Hegel's ideals and emphasis on universality, they ascribed to the assumption of the superiority of the West over other cultures. The twentieth century ushered in new levels of horror and vexation, and in the midst arose a philosopher who explored landmark ideas while aligning them with dubious public policies. Heidegger's shadow is a long and wide one that challenges reflection on several levels. The addendum explores those issues in greater detail. The main text will delve into his contribution and address his perplexing actions and views.

One of the challenges in evaluating art is its vast diversity, which leads some to conclude that there are no standards and no methods of evaluation. For example, consider the differences between a painting by Rembrandt and Carl Andre's work, *Equivalent VIII* (1966). The latter sculpture is sometimes referred to as *The Bricks*. Both are art made by artists even though their work is a study in contrast. When I mention the arts, I am thinking about work created by people, people who call themselves artists because they make art. Nature is also beautiful, but it is not art. Nature, according to most religions, has a divine creator and has its own wonders. Art is created by human beings. Thus, this book focuses on work created by people.

The additional challenge for people in the arts is often called social relevancy. Does art help feed the world? Make us more peaceful? Teach us citizenship? Or is it oblivious to world hunger, violence, and oppression? Some of those issues will be addressed with hints, suggestions, and proposals outlined in the pages that follow.

1

Historical Considerations

Art has the power to generate heated debates, pensive moods, or restless indifference. Because of our varied reactions, art might fascinate us and, at the same time, challenge us to think in new ways. Because art influences our views when we encounter a new work, do we need to listen and observe, understand our own feelings, and form innovative ideas from that experience? Art is sometimes considered dangerous and, at other times, an asset to society. Do those emotional responses indicate whether a work is good, bad, or just irrelevant to life? We will consider why some wish to censor the arts while others advocate all expressions, even controversial works.

When we study the arts, what exactly are we studying? Is there "content" in art, or is it just emotional release and pleasure? There is no parallel between the content of science and the arts. Both work in their own ways. And although a work of art can be studied through certain tools of scientific and statistical analysis, seldom does anyone judge its value based on scientific methods. As Linda Shaver-Gleason observes, "We don't need science to tell us why a Mozart is great; we only need to listen to one measure."[1]

1. Shaver-Gleason, "You Don't Need Science to Tell You Why You Like a Song." Online.

The relationship between the fields of art and science is complicated. Advocates for the arts often claim that the arts are essential for science, but science is not essential for the study of art. In her essay, Anna Powers makes the case that new insights in science depend on an aesthetic view and not just empirical research.[2] Art is the process of engaging the imagination—which is also a requirement for science.

A major challenge artists face is the accusation that the arts are irrelevant and even indifferent to the needs of the world, whereas science is relevant and far from indifferent. The ideas we gain from science are important, but as Albert Einstein reminds us,

> We do science when we reconstruct in the language of logic what we have seen and experienced; we do art when we communicate through forms whose connections are not accessible to the conscious mind, yet we intuitively recognize them as something meaningful."[3]

The domain of the arts, intuition, feelings, and a search for meaning are also components of science. The arts have a vital function in many social, educational, and economic systems. Can you imagine a business without any advertising? Packaging? Office decor? Artists create those. Television shows would not exist without costumes, sets, makeup, light, and audio designers. And even though it is not always evident, vocal training also matters for any public figure. And it is comforting to know that Einstein acknowledges the importance of experience for science. The arts form many of those experiences in our lives. Because time and space are limited, as well as my training, we will focus on the arts and not the beauty that is inherent in scientific thinking. In that sense, science invokes knowledge, and art evokes wisdom.

Art evokes responses from its audience in surprising ways that are usually constructive but can also disrupt. People often react to theatre performances in a deeply personal way. Reactions to theatre productions are often so personal that many believe no

2. Powers, "Why Art Is Vital to The Study of Science."
3. Albert Einstein, quoted in Caglioti, "Art according to Albert Einstein."

two people can ever respond in the same way. Discussions following productions often support that view since many, including the friend sitting next to you, mentions things that only they experienced. Since there is such a diversity of reactions, how can single, let alone multiple works, ever receive general acclaim or wide endorsement? This brief essay will explore those themes and suggest that the diversity of responses reveals the strength of the work.

Art creates "aesthetic" experiences. What does that mean? First, it is not a formula or a logical process. An artwork is an object but also more than that. Something beyond the work itself happens to create an aesthetic experience. The aesthetic experience begins with a work of art, but it doesn't end there. Material is needed to make a work of art, but the work of art evokes a response that is not made of material. Our reactions to artworks are often emotional or reflective. A work of art might be a play in performance, but the work of art also includes what *effect* it has on those who experience it. Art, at its best, creates responses called aesthetic moments, which can deeply impact the individual and larger segments of society. What art does is individual and subjective, whereas a work of art is generally objective material: wind, wood, reeds, and metal needed for many orchestral instruments. Dance requires the dancer's body. Even art stored on the ethernet requires complex physical systems ranging from electrical to memory storage to programming.

The work that art does is to create the aesthetic moment. Such an experience might last only a moment, but it has the power to focus emotions and thoughts to make it memorable. Do you recall plays, music, or other artworks that you enjoyed? Why do we remember those events and forget what we ate last week? Is food not as important as art? Often, people distinctly recall a "before" and "after" an encounter with a work of art. Such events are vivid. The idea is that, subjectively, we remember notable artistic experiences because they change our understanding of self and awareness of others. Once you have seen a Rembrandt, can you easily forget it? That is why people often want to talk with one another after they have seen an emotionally packed movie. Some of the writers in this study observed that art is not unique because other ways of knowing—theology, medicine, science, or any other quest—also create memorable experiences. Other fields of study might debate this point. We could investigate how the arts challenge religious and other academic pursuits, but that is not the aim of this book. The art we experience enables reflection and analysis because art is more than paint on a canvas; it is a search for truth and beauty. That is the assumption for this text.

Aesthetic moments are those markers in time when things change inside and around you. If you attend a play or concert, suddenly, you feel yourself transported away from the seat into another sphere. You look around, and everyone seems to have a new radiance. Your feet feel as though they have lifted you up onto a new level, and yet you have not left your seat. It is possible the people around you feel just as they did before.

But you, the viewer, have changed. The moment will be memorable because there was a before and an after. Again, name a painting, poem, or movie that caught your attention twenty years ago. Even though the full meaning of that first encounter may not be comprehended at the moment, the memory will dwell inside and continue to impact your responses to further experiences. If you see a Vincent van Gogh painting, what happens if you see another one? Based on this theory, I suggest that you might have a sense of joy or pleasure that comes with the recognition of the artist's style or theme. This might also occur with music, theatre, or any other art medium. If someone claims that this joy of recognition, of dwelling in a work, has never happened to them, I often reply, just wait, just wait, it will. Even the ancients were aware of this phenomenon.

Plato

The two philosophers who initiated the discussion of the arts and their impact on the soul were Plato (427–317 BCE) and his student Aristotle (384–322 BCE). Plato had serious doubts about whether art could benefit civil society. For that reason, he sought to ban most of it. Still, Plato found a few art forms that might be useful.[4] Music, he reasoned, with its emphasis on strong harmony, can help people subdue their emotions and develop calm and reasonable personalities. Mathematics, he said, is even better than music because it teaches people eternal concepts such as $2 + 2 = 4$ and $2 \times 2 = 4$, not to mention logic. We can envision the perfect triangle, Plato insists, but in the material realm, no perfect triangle exists. Ideas transcend all material forms, which, in the end, are but copies of what resides eternally. This idea of beauty is still pervasive in many cultures. Abstract painter Mark Rothko notes, "Our notions of beauty today are essentially Platonic."[5] And that is not a compliment. He objects to the rebirth of idealism in our culture. Rothko's quest was to bring back expressiveness by means of abstract painting. Colors, his paintings attest, were his medium of expression.

The arts, according to Plato, that never reach the level of eternal ideals include cooking, cosmetics, painting, poetry, and theatre. That is quite a list! Cooking involves the preparation of material items to serve the material needs of humans; as such, it can never rise to meet ideal standards. Painting essentially functions at the same level. People paint portraits, landscapes, houses, or animals and deploy materials in the making. However, using material to reproduce the appearance of a material object on canvas means that painting will never rise to the level of the ideal. Plato argues that an imitation of an imitation cannot convey truth. But by far the worst forms of so-called art are poetry and theatre. Poetry, Plato contends, exists primarily to express emotions, and emotions are usually chaotic and, therefore, far from any ideal. And like theatre, poetry has a pretense of telling you the truth when it is the opposite. Theatre is too emotional to approximate any ideal and, even more damning, it encourages sentiments that, in Plato's view, are "womanly virtues" (such as wailing) but do not meet the decorum required of men. Go to a play, Plato says, and you will see grown men cry. What an embarrassment! What a confusion of

4. Plato, *Republic,*, Book 10.
5. Rothko, *The Artist's Reality*, 67.

gender identities! Plato is deeply troubled that people are willing to applaud such deceptions.

Plato introduced the idea that theatre brings pleasure and that pleasure is essential for a population to enjoy their city.[6] And he continues that the arts may have a place in the city if a common "canon" is created. "In this way, the city and citizens enjoy the same pleasures and can live well and happily."[7] The political authorities should be granted the right to create such a canon. Plato places considerable trust in the political arena as the place where the arts are to be judged as acceptable or rejected as problematic. The artist who brings pleasure through performance needs to work within the limits of social and political standards. In ideal situations, this is how art functions in society. For Plato, a good state needs good art to sustain a high degree of social harmony. And since kings, especially philosopher kings, understand how to create harmony, they should be recognized as the ultimate arbiters for judging art. For the state, art will contribute to the ethical and patriotic ideals that all should strive to attain.

Plato's idealism can be illustrated by acknowledging that every person has a mental image of an ideal fish, pet, work of art, or government. But the *actual* fish, work of art, pet, or government is always a flawed imitation. Nothing that is made of material can become ideal, and social institutions are made of human material. There are just a few disciplines that come close to approximating the ideal. Mathematics has a degree of precision and, therefore, informs us of an ideal formula. Harmonies in music can be so good that they remind us of perfection. A government, if managed by a philosopher king, can also approximate but never completely attain the political ideal. Since ideals are eternal, they are also universal: the ideal does not change colors when it crosses language barriers. But the arts, sadly, for Plato, are not just an imitation of an ideal, but they are imitations of imitations. The actor might be entertaining but can only achieve an imitation of other humans who act in imitation of their ideals, at best, or faulty actions, at

6. Plato, *Laws*, 88.

7. Plato, *Laws*, 281.

worst. Still, in spite of this, there is some hope for the arts. If artists advocate political ideals, then the state can tolerate and laud the artist. Good theatre will teach duty and loyalty and steer people away from emotions and pleasures. The philosopher king will allow only dutiful theatre and ban the emotional performances that seem so typical of Greek theatre.

For Plato, philosophy is superior to math because, with the study of philosophy, a person can learn eternal ideas. In the realm of ideas, there are never shades of gray: freedom is always freedom, duty is duty, and greed is always greed. Those ideas never change and have never changed, according to Plato. But the most perfect ideal on earth would be a city ruled by a philosopher king. Since philosophy provides humans with eternal thoughts, the king makes political decisions based on the best ideas.

In his earlier work, *Republic*,[8] Plato outlined his plan for the ideal state. Theatre, and all the arts, did not fare well in that work. When people attend plays, for example, they will imitate the immoral behavior they have witnessed by actors. And because the theatre presents despicable characters (consider Macbeth, for example), it is possible that the theatre will corrupt the public. Presenting ill deeds on stage will not improve the state.[9] Therefore, plays need to be banned or rewritten to show good men and women doing good deeds. But who can find such a play?

A governmental ban on theatre was successfully implemented by the British Puritans during the Interregnum. Their arguments for the closure were two-fold. First, actors must say character's lines that are not their own words, and thus, they deceive the public with lies. Secondly, the theatres are a bad influence because they teach people to laugh, and laughter is an offense to God. The Puritans forcibly tore down the theatres and sold the timbers to the neglected poor. Theatre artists fled to France to avoid arrest. That included William D'Avenant, who was a Royalist who opposed Oliver Cromwell's Puritan Commonwealth. Attempting to flee England, he was captured and imprisoned in the

8. Plato, *Republic*, 79–104.

9. "Acts and Ordinances of the Interregnum, 1642–1660."

Tower of London.[10] While in prison, he wrote performance pieces that emphasized morality, including his five-volume patriotic work, *Gondibert: An Heroick Poem* (1651). Other works followed, which focused on good characters who did good and noble deeds. He was widely read, and some of his productions were performed at Rutland House with invited audiences. He was released from prison and, after the Restoration in 1660, continued to write eight adaptations of Shakespeare. D'Avenant's career illustrates the reality that governments can stifle and even close theatres, although eventually, the arts break through barriers and thrive again.

The characters in both tragedies and comedies teach the public that lying is acceptable since, by acting, they do not present their true selves but a fabrication. "Let us have no more lies of that sort,"[11] Plato insists. Then he continues: "If anyone at all is to have the privilege of lying, the rulers of the State should be those persons."[12] Because the actor pretends to be someone he is not (actors were all male in Greek theatre, and likewise in England until the advent of Restoration drama in 1660), citizens will be encouraged to take on personages they are not. A person cannot be a serious person if he learns to act as another character with conviction. Tragedy, Plato argues, misleads the public by teaching them that good men should imitate women and freely show their emotions. A good character on stage would be worthy of imitation, but sadly, according to Plato, the poets of ancient Greece did not agree. And just when you think the rules are too stringent, Plato adds this prescription concerning music: "There remain only the lyre and the harp for use in a city."[13] In the country, he would permit the pipe.

---

10. For a synopsis of D'Avenant's career during and after the Interregnum, see "William Davenant," and for a record of D'Avenant's writing output (poetry, plays, histories), a rather comprehensive bibliography is available at *Online Books by William D'Avenant (D'Avenant, William, 1606–1668)*.

11. Plato, *Republic*, 79.

12. Plato, *Republic*, 86.

13. Plato, *Republic*, 102.

Aristotle

Aristotle begins his discussion where Plato also began: the arts offer pleasure. There are differences in how people experience artistic pleasure, and Aristotle analyzes why that is so. He begins by dissecting plays, how they produce pleasure, and how they impact individual and community life. If Plato is correct that a common artistic experience can help create a happy citizenry, Aristotle raises the question of how that happens. Plato was interested in a predictable result; Aristotle was interested in the process. Plato recommended that the aim of theatre be civic harmony; Aristotle investigates what is necessary to create harmony. One might say the two ancients began on the same foot but leaped in different directions.

For Aristotle, knowledge is gained by observing phenomena. Therefore, the study of all things that are material is essential. It is not enough to know how to go fishing; it is better to notice the different kinds of aquatic life and to identify each kind. Art and theatre originate as material objects and need to be observed at that level, although everyone knows their content is not limited to the material. With theatre, Aristotle observes that it has distinct component parts: plot, character, language, rhythm, music, and spectacle. He lists these in the order of importance, with spectacle as the least valuable for a play. Then, he discusses how they function to create an effect on the audience.

Theatre works because it is based upon imitation. But it is not a simple imitation, as in trying to shoot an arrow the way you see someone else do it. Aristotle asks, why shoot an arrow? What is your purpose? That, to Aristotle, becomes an imitation of an action.[14] The best characters in a play imitate not the physical business but the actions of a person. Action, for Aristotle, means the dynamic that makes the person do what they do. Centuries later, Dylan Thomas would identify it as "The force that through the green fuse drives the flower."[15] Imitating action is thus integral to a

---

14. Aristotle, *Poetics*, 17f.
15. Thomas, "The Force That through the Green Fuse Drives the Flower."

play. With that thought in mind, let us turn to an example of a play by Sophocles, *Antigone*.

Why does Antigone do what she does? That information is vital to understanding her character. What drives her determination to bury her brother Polyneices after the king has forbidden it? Why does a person engage in civil disobedience? She does it because the gods demand the burial of a family member. The fact that Creon, the king, has threatened the death penalty to anyone who buries Polyneices does not deter her. In that act, we learn to know Antigone's character and may also understand we might become like her—by obeying gods rather than kings. By rejecting the king's command, she disobeys the state. What drives Antigone to civil disobedience? Her religion and her bonds with her family. She does not wish to violate these commitments. Her act is an imitation rooted in love for her brother and duty to the gods. In contrast with her brothers, who killed each other in battle, Antigone presents a character who employs nonviolent resistance. Keep that in mind: the ancients knew of nonviolent resistance! And in the case of Sophocles, they advocated it. Antigone resisted authority while fully cognizant of the consequences of her actions. Execution awaited her.

For Aristotle, examples such as Antigone illustrate imitation as the highest form of personal and dramatic integrity. With the application of that term, he upends Plato's idealism and places the focus of the arts on the shoulders of all humans. Once we have seen a character in action, we become responsible for what we have learned in that encounter. In this sense, Aristotle links aesthetics with ethics.

Aristotle acknowledges that we are not all born with the same sense of pleasure. We have differing perceptions of that basic consideration. Because people have diverse views, it is important for a play to provide a common experience. That experience, he says, begins with a plot that draws us into the story and characters with whom we empathize. A play requires language that stimulates our minds and a rhythm that provides a unifying tempo. And, finally, he suggests, sometimes a spectacle will surprise even the most jaded. But Aristotle was careful about spectacle. He cautioned that it might dominate a production and prove to be a distraction from the essential elements. Examples of spectacle that might be appropriate include the sudden appearance of a *deus ex machina* or, at the end of *Oedipus*, the main character with a mask that shows his blinded, bloody eyes.

Theatre relies on imitation, and without that, it devolves into recital and fails as theatre. Imitation of an action means, for Aristotle, a character's objective and the decisions they make to achieve that goal. In a comedy, those decisions slowly solve the tension in the play, and in a tragedy, the opposite occurs. "Tragedy, then, is an imitation of an action that is serious, complete, and of a certain magnitude; in language embellished with each kind of artistic ornament, the several kinds being found in separate parts of the play; in the form of action, not of narrative; through pity and fear affecting the proper purgation of these emotions."[16] Think about that. A tragedy releases us from fear and pity, which Aristotle identifies as the most powerful and crippling of all emotions. When we become free from them, we become whole again. That is catharsis. Catharsis is not a pleasant feeling, a feeling of bliss, but, in fact, the process of restoring people and society to wholeness. Making people emotionally whole is the function of theatre, according to Aristotle. If we are crippled by fear or guilt, we will not be able to participate in society with a sense of freedom. When someone is not free, relating to others becomes a dreaded chore.

When the elements of a play are effectively staged, Aristotle refers to that as the tying and untying of the plot.[17] The audience becomes empathetic with the characters and is drawn deeper and deeper into the complexities of the plot when the surprise occurs: a climactic moment. There is the setup when Tiresias tells Oedipus that he is the grown man who was predicted to engage in great sins (*hamartia*), which are now the cause of the famine. The climactic turn occurs when Oedipus realizes the truth of that statement and must now act to punish not some wayward citizen but himself,

16. Aristotle, *Poetics*, 45.

17. Aristotle, *Poetics*, 25–30.

the king. At that moment, all the pent-up emotions of the plot are released in sorrow because we have empathized so much with the king.

With the revelation from Tiresias, the king now despises himself, and we share his grief. Aristotle calls that moment catharsis. The chaos is now explained, disorder in the city can return to order, and the twisted riddle of the famine is untied. Catharsis marks an aesthetic experience, a moment of heightened pleasure, and we are made whole again, once more able to participate in society, free from fear and self-pity. This insight needs careful attention: aesthetic moments free us from fear and guilt so we can be active citizens again. Freedom, according to Aristotle's *Poetics*, means we are free from fear and guilt. It was often said of the late congressman John Lewis that he was unafraid of the police batons or dogs that attacked the marchers on Edmund Pettis Bridge in Alabama in 1965. He tasted freedom as the freedom from fear. President F. D. Roosevelt had made the same point more than thirty years earlier in his First Inaugural Address: "The only thing we have to fear is fear itself."

With his work in *Poetics*, Aristotle left Plato's idealism behind. Instead, his empirical method became dominant in aesthetic analysis. Artists, critics, and patrons generally agree that the arts should avoid the pretense of expressing ideals. Plato's method is decisive when authoritarian political systems control a society. Aristotle's method has tended to be more effective when political systems try to address social needs. Plato gave students of the arts objective measures to evaluate any given work: does it teach ideals? Aristotle's analysis examines how the arts impact the individual and society. That is roughly how the differences between the two philosophical methods have divided Western society, religion, politics, and education for centuries.

Empiricism and its method are a challenge for many today. Some wish to hold on to former beliefs that science challenges. Others are uninformed as to how scientific procedures work, and still others believe that the mythical and mystical provide greater truths than science. But while the power of myth has its place in the human community, it needs to be said that now and then, myths require evaluation. This is a quite different emphasis from Plato's notion of eternal, unchanging ideas from the alpha to the omega.

Six hundred years after Plato, as Christianity spread through the Northern Mediterranean area, the philosopher's idealism was integrated by Augustine (354–430 CE) into orthodox Christian doctrine and religious language. Augustine did not hesitate to take Plato's perfect "idea" and apply that concept to a perfect God, a blameless Jesus, and the perfected community—which, for Augustine, was the monastery. In sum, Augustine sought to use Plato's philosophy and gave it a Christian blessing. For that reason, he advocated the suppression of emotions and the necessity of banning the arts that evoke emotional responses. He wrote only one short treatise on music and nothing on visual arts. His merging of Plato's thought with Christian doctrine left the church at large to assume that he accepted Plato's views on the arts overall. But instead of proposing with Plato that the republic has the right to ban some of the arts, he placed the church at the center of life, and therefore, the church asserted that central role.[18] Augustine encouraged art forms that would suppress the heart and challenge the mind to think about things eternal, such as mathematics, pure harmony in music, and philosophy. The bishop of Rome now functioned as the theological monarch to serve everyone for the betterment of humanity. Challenges to the bishop's authority and medieval Christianity began to emerge with some regularity.

Thomas Aquinas

One priest who developed an alternative approach was the Italian Thomas Aquinas (1225–74), who spent much of his adult life teaching theology at the University of Paris.[19] He wrote extensively on theology but also a long treatise on beauty, which he considered to be a division of theology and not a secular area of thought. We

18. "Augustinian Platonism," *Encyclopedia Britannica*.

19. Sevier, *Aquinas on Beauty*, 255ff.

need to recall that he lived during the building of the great cathedrals. Chartres Cathedral, for example, was completed in 1252, a period that saw the development of stained glass. Large flat glass sheets had not been invented yet, so small globs of glass were fastened in place with lead bands. Then, dyes were added to the glass, and cathedral builders quickly adapted that invention. Aquinas's treatise on art is a study of stained glass: not the images or figures one can make with the assorted colors but the colors themselves. His question, to put it simply, was how can light, which we cannot see, become light that we can see? How does color do that? He did not go far into the science of optics, but his empirical curiosity led him to make a few poignant observations. How can light, which is invisible, pass through glass and possess the color of that glass—and yet the colors do not disappear from the glass?

The colors that shine through those windows bring clarity to light itself. The primary function of art is thus *to bring clarity*. Johnny Nash's popular song, "I can see clearly now," would be consistent with Aquinas's thought. The premise is that art clarifies not just light but human experience and the perceptions of the divine. That is the value of art.

Aquinas provided answers to his questions, but the answers are not exactly scientific. In the way that invisible light passes through the glass and becomes visible, also holds true for the divine-human connection. When the invisible God passes through us, we, too, can become beautiful in word and deed. We can wear the colors of divinity when we recognize that light from above came to earth to shine through us onto the world. And just like the glass, our good deeds do not dim the light we have in us. We cannot see through the stained glass in the windows to see what is on the other side. In the same way, we cannot see the source of the light that shines on us. We must accept it in the same way that salvation comes to all who let their light shine. When the colors of the windows shine on us, we take on those colors. Light becomes the metaphor for Aquinas's understanding of divine presence.

That is then true for other arts as well. We cannot see spoken words, yet they exist when uttered. We cannot see what we smell, and yet the odors are real. We cannot hear light or odors, but we can hear music, and that, too, is a mystery. How can something we cannot see become a sound that we hear? Aquinas does not have scientific answers, but to him, that is not necessary. What is essential is that all the senses are ways through which the divine can reach us. Thus, life is our chance to pay attention and bathe ourselves in the beauty of color.

That is where things stood until the Enlightenment, which, in the field of aesthetics, might also be identified as the age of integrative thought. The new methodology combining Plato's idealism with Aristotle's empiricism did not spring forth overnight. It was a gradual development that began with the discovery of some of Aristotle's writings and their embrace by Thomas Aquinas. Aquinas sought an empirical approach to theology and, eventually, aesthetics, and he referred to both as divine sciences. While he significantly influenced theology, his influence on aesthetics was less pronounced. Aquinas considered the beautiful and the good to have great similarities. The good is what people do, and the beautiful is what people perceive. Our perceptions come to us via the senses (sight, sound, touch), but we give them meaning by awareness and then thought. And it is in the realm of thought that a good deed and a good work of art become indistinguishable.[20] The difference is in how we become aware of each: reason for one, sensual encounter for the other. It was German philosopher Immanuel Kant who took on the task of finding a middle ground between reason and sensation.

Immanuel Kant

Immanuel Kant (1724–1804) neither diminished nor lauded idealism or empiricism for his aesthetics. He avoided the discussion of imitation and found a way to link ethics with aesthetics. To achieve this, he developed a new methodology that he called subjective disinterestedness and subjective universality. He acknowledged

---

20. Aquinas, "Beauty Is a Kind of Knowledge."

the place of emotions (Aristotle) and a route toward a universal (Plato) analysis without recreating the dichotomy left in their wake. The judgment of art, he declared, can only happen by persons who have no ulterior interest in the arts. What he meant is that responding to art should be free from political, economic, religious, and moral interests. Only those free from those interests when they experience a work of art, can be counted on as dependable respondents and critics. The theatre owner who has invested in a production is not a dependable judge, and neither is the pastor who wants to know if the play teaches moral truths. In other words, Kant proposed that art should be evaluated for art's sake. This raises the question: what, for Kant, is art's sake?

Aristotle emphasized that persons who have been released by catharsis from fear and guilt will be free to live in harmony. Kant emphasized that those who approach art with disinterestedness will be free to experience what the artwork actually is. In those moments, the artwork itself guides us toward an aesthetic moment unlike all other experiences in life—because it enables us to experience the sublime. For Kant, there are two kinds of sublime, specifically the mathematical and the artistic. Here, we will examine what he meant by the sublime in art.

The sublime occurs, according to Kant, when our experience of art stimulates the interplay of our "faculties"—a mutual stimulation of both imagination and knowledge. Kant also noted that when our imaginations experience "free play," they are on the verge of creating innovative ideas on a cognitive level. Interplay and free play are subjective occurrences that evoke an emotional response and an intellectual one. When both the intellect and emotions react to a work of art, we have an aesthetic moment. This is not a passive experience but one that provokes internal and often external action. And it all begins with an artistic creation that initiates our response. Aesthetic moments provide a deep sense of pleasure, which results in outward action. In that sense, Kant proposed that the beautiful and the morally good have great similarities. Learning to understand what makes an artwork good will help us understand how people are good. By learning how to make an artwork, we will have a better understanding of others who create good things or practice good deeds. They are not identical, but when we see a good deed, we may react in a way that is similar to responding to a good play. So, what is a good play?

Identifying an excellent work of art is far more complicated for Kant than having it meet ideals (Plato) or creating a production that evokes catharsis (Aristotle).[21] A work of art may be devoid of ideals and catharsis. Yet a work of art may have a significant agenda as an expression of truth. When the experience of a work of art, our imagination, and our knowledge all coalesce into a new awareness, we are on the verge of recognizing truth in ways we had not considered before. For example, Hamlet wildly thrusts his sword into the window arras, and then we watch as Polonius emerges, fatally wounded. That has perhaps made generations of viewers more cautious about making rash decisions. Though a work of art may seem ugly, unfit, or unsuitable for society, it may yet have great aesthetic value. It may reveal to us the truth we have been avoiding, denying, or rejecting. Some art will disturb us in that way because it incites the interplay of our imagination with our knowledge. Knowledge is the foundation, of course, but without imagination, it becomes routine and banal. By the same token, imagination is also a human asset, but without knowledge, it can easily become unmoored and float away from reality.

Therefore, art that provokes a response is revealing the truth. Art that does not could then be considered bad art. Bad art is that which fails to evoke a reaction. The more intense the response, the more meaningful the work. But that is subjective and does not constitute a universal judgment of the work itself. To arrive at a universal judgment requires more than an individual, subjective response to a work of art. Accordingly, who can ever decide whether a work of art has any value if even "ugly" works contribute to our lives? Because responses are subjective, there are no criteria for evaluating whether your response is a good or inadequate one. Your response is valid for you. So how can anyone ever decide whether certain works have greater meaning or value than others?

21. Kant, *Critique of Judgment*, 10.

You like this music, I do not, but who am I to disagree with you? To solve that problem of extremely subjective taste in the arts, Kant introduced *a priori* categories of time and space.[22] A work of art exists in space, and repeated experiences of that same work illustrate how it exists through time. The repeated exposure to that same work will inform our judgment. Eventually, we may love a painting more than we did the first time, or sometimes the opposite effect occurs. Some plays, such as Hermann Sudermann's *Magda* (1893), created a huge sensation in their social and political milieu but are no longer perceived as particularly dynamic. Once the social and political conditions described in the play cease to exist, the play can lose its impact. Some works are so dependent on the crises of their time that when those issues fade, the work loses vitality. In 1966, the musical *Viet Rock* repeatedly drew huge audiences. It was an imaginative, antiwar rock musical by Megan Terry. This Open Theatre production became the precursor to counter-culture productions, including *Hair.* Now, that time has passed, along with love beads and bell bottoms. Works that span time and across language barriers continue to provoke an emotional response. They will be judged as better than other works that were completely topical in their moment but now rest in the dustbin of history. Durability becomes essential, not just over one person's lifetime or within one cultural context.

Kant was also adamant in pointing out that art and science are two different modes of thinking. Science demands singular and correct answers. $E=mc^2$ is the formula that can destroy a city, but $D=mc^2$ is meaningless. Art, on the other hand, has a multitude of configurations and will generate multiple responses. The greater the variability in reactions means that work has universality. When many disagree about the work of art, and that work continues to generate disagreement, the work is usually better than works that generate uniform responses. Ongoing disagreement and critical discussion in the present and over a span of time signifies durability.

22. Kant, *Critique of Judgment*, 15.

Thus, for Kant, art stimulates the perception of difference on two levels. First, a variety of reactions is desirable. Second, observing differences is the beginning of knowledge. If you can distinguish a wren from a sparrow, you have learned something. Kant's emphasis on the diversity of reactions still has currency today. Consider the observation by the Abstract Expressionist painter Mark Rothko. "Every (artistic) shape becomes an organic entity, inviting a multiplicity of associations inherent in all living things."[23] Science, on the other hand, depends on singular, correct responses. But science often thrives with the second principle above observing differences. The same can be said to be true in the arts also. Learning to distinguish a Rembrandt from a Vermeer is foundational for art history.

Furthermore, those who devote their time and effort to the study of durable works will have a more universal understanding of art. For example, William Shakespeare was not the most popular playwright of his time, but by now, he has emerged as the definitive playwright of his era. Immersion in the arts and not popularity is the preparation for evaluating art. Therefore, those individuals will have a trained subjective response because they are familiar with how a work might transcend itself through time, space, and across cultures. With this last step, Kant created the art critic! The person immersed in theatre or music will be a more dependable judge of a work of theatre or music. This begins to sound like a new hierarchy where some subjective reactions are superior to other subjective responses. And that is what he intends. Even though he emphasizes democratic subjectivity, the critic is born by adding the final criteria that immersion trains subjectivity. And in general, this is a popular view. If you had a choice of weighing the subjective responses to a new play and you were asked to compare responses by Lin-Manuel Miranda and the president of J. P. Morgan, which one would you choose? Even though they both might write well and be truthful about their subjective reactions, it is likely you would place a higher value on the comments by the creator of *Hamilton*. Why? According to Kant, immersion over

23. . Rothko, *Writings on Art*, 48.

time trains our subjective responses. Education, to say it another way, impacts judgment. The dilemma is that the artist would like everyone to love their work! Yet maybe only a few will be able to evaluate it.

Immanuel Kant changed the direction of the debate between the Platonists and Aristotelians, but he did not end it. Even though Kant was limited to his Prussian world and Western philosophy, his emphasis on the multiplicity of interpretations introduces the possibility that great works of art will embody diversity. With that emphasis, he leaned toward the empirical method (Aristotle) even though he assumed that the arts could express ideals (the aesthetic good). Kant opened the windows to another approach, and G. W. F. Hegel recognized it immediately.

G. W. F. Hegel

G. W. F. Hegel (1770–1830) followed Kant with another new proposal. His four-volume work, *The Philosophy of Fine Art*, outlines an ambitious approach that integrates Plato's eternal idea and Aristotle's emotional experience. He proposed that instead of bypassing the categories established by the two ancients, the opposing views could be examined as a dialectic in search of a synthesis.[24] For Hegel, the idealism of Plato serves as the thesis in the dialectic, and Aristotle's empiricism is the antithesis. The clash between these two results in a synthesis which unites them as one.

Hegel presents a challenge for anyone who tries to write a summary of his system of thought. The first challenge is that he integrates a philosophy of art with a philosophy of history to such an extent that one is dependent on the other. Second, for the first time in the history of philosophy, Hegel attempts to explain how idealism and empiricism are both required to formulate an aesthetic. This perspective begins with an idea, a concept that is the thesis in his dialectic. Since every thesis requires an antithesis, empirical analysis serves that purpose. The struggle between thesis and

24. Beardsley, *Aesthetics: A Short History*, 257f.

antithesis is resolved with a new synthesis, and in that moment, the moment of integration, the transcendent spirit moves history forward. History moves forward with a new thesis that conflicts with a new antithesis, which is then only resolved with another synthesis. Without this struggle, Hegel argues, history would not exist, and in fact, it would end.[25] And art would not exist because art is the dynamic that moves this dialectic forward. Consider the civil rights movement in the 1950s and 1960s. Every mass rally was infused with civil rights songs, including those by Pete Seeger, Odetta, and Joan Baez.

With Hegel in mind, we can usefully revisit Sophocles' ancient tragedy *Antigone* (fifth century BCE). Hegel designates the play as the best example of a dialectic struggle. "Dramatic poetry must be regarded as the highest phase of poetry."[26] The city of Thebes had experienced famine and hunger, which eventually led to Oedipus's choice of self-imposed exile. That was followed by a civil war initiated by his sons, Eteocles and Polyneices. The complication in the play is that the twin sons of Oedipus were supposed to trade rulership of the city, back and forth between the two of them after Oedipus exiled himself. Eteocles was supposed to rule for seven years and then yield the city to Polyneices, who would rule for the next seven. But Eteocles refused to cede the throne, which is why Polyneices attacked. Both died in that war. At the beginning of the play, the new king, Creon, has declared that the twin brother who died defending the city shall have an honorable burial while the other twin who attacked the city shall have his body exposed to the elements. That was a legal declaration by the king, which established the thesis. And Creon threatens that if anyone violates this pronouncement, they will be put to death.

The antithesis is then introduced by Antigone, who recognizes the power of the king and his edict but takes as her guide a higher law: what the gods require when a family member dies is a proper burial. She pours a handful of dirt on the body of Polyneices and is arrested: a synthesis. According to Creon's way of thinking,

25. Fukuyama, *The End of History and the Last Man*, 59–69.
26. Hegel, *Philosophy of Fine Art*, vol. IV, 248.

the city's problems are resolved. However, he does not count on his son, Haemon, who is in love with Antigone and opposes the arrest and threatens to die with her. This establishes a new thesis. Creon makes light of Haemon's threat as the antithesis. Enter the prophet Tiresias, who introduces another synthesis by recognizing Creon's authority and, at the same time, warns him that his unwise edict will bring destruction to his home. It is unwise because Creon has positioned himself and his laws above the gods, and thus, punishment will ensue. Creon must decide quickly. He orders the release of Antigone (thesis) but is soon informed by a messenger that Antigone hung herself in her cell (antithesis). Creon is now desperate to reverse his decision to save the life of Haemon (attempted synthesis), who has disappeared. But a shepherd arrives who tells of the death of Haemon by his own sword (another antithesis). And just when Creon thinks he cannot endure any more punishment, praying for mercy from the gods, he hears a scream inside the palace. A servant rushes out to tell him that his wife, Eurydice, has taken her own life. The only synthesis now available is exile for Creon—so that the city can finally end the chaos that began when fate visited the house of Argos.

Antigone illustrates Hegel's method of analysis.[27] The thesis, Creon's edict, is an idea that is challenged by Antigone's material actions: the burial of Polyneices. The synthesis occurs when the "spirit" intervenes, and the narrative advances to a synthesis, which becomes the next thesis. That process, where material realities challenge concepts, explains the function of art in history. What the artist creates, from the raw materials of existence, forces a change in perception, which then leads to new knowledge. Therefore, what the artist does is create the dynamics that lead to historical change. Those changes, Hegel assumed, would result in higher levels of justice, devotion, and understanding. Simply stated, Rosalind Franklin's discovery of the double-helix structure of the molecule led to new knowledge about chromosomes that encode genetic information.[28] In this way, history advances

27. Hegel, *Philosophy of Fine Art*, vol. I, 293ff.

28. "Rosalind Franklin," *Encyclopedia Britannica*,

as material realities shape new ideas, which then lead to the discovery of new material realities, and the dialectical process begins again. Art and the material discoveries created by the artist are among the forces that propel history forward. In that sense, art defines the *spirit of an age*. The classical world is known for the art—poetry, theatre, architecture, and visual arts—it created. As Leo Tolstoy interpreted him, Hegel thought of beauty as the breaking of God into history.[29] When the two conflicting forces, thesis, and antithesis, resolve with a new synthesis, that is how the spirit (*Geist*) breaks into history.

Hegel's view is that politics is the art of governing. But those in charge need to pay attention to the material needs of the governed. Politics that ignores those needs will be challenged by material shortcomings, which will force change. The arts originate, on the one hand, at the level of material need, while at the same time, the abundance or shortage of materials to meet those needs will alter people's thoughts on religion, law, politics, and the arts. During times of unmet needs, the arts become bolder in their critique of society. And so, according to Hegel, art bends history toward justice. Plays such as *Antigone* change our understanding of political decrees and how we view those who act for justice amid a crisis. With his dialectic in mind, it is understandable that in a society where orthodoxy is the thesis, new theatre works will present the antithesis and thereby challenge conventional thought. The artist pushes history forward by not allowing the thesis to rest on its laurels. New works always challenge prior artistic forms and styles.

Hegel also advanced the discussion by emphasizing the importance of historical context for art. Art is not created in a vacuum but originates from the artist's response to social, political, and religious circumstances. Any analysis of art must take into consideration the conditions of the era in which the artist works. That is why ancient classical art differs so much from contemporary work. And it explains why not all cultures can be judged by European criteria for the arts.[30] Without using the term,

29. Tolstoy, *What Is Art?*, 23.
30. Hegel, *On Art, Religion, Philosophy*, 45f.

Hegel makes a case for diversity in the arts by highlighting the importance of historical and cultural context. The "spirit" that creates the dynamic that propels history is present in all cultures—it is not limited to Western civilization. (Although the Christian West, Hegel believed, has advantages over other cultures. His emphasis on the spirit inherent in each culture may have opened the door to subsequent distortions by the National Socialists.)

The question that emerges is why artists do what they do and what components are needed.[31] Kant called it genius. Hegel adds to that view. An artist must begin with a desire. Hegel calls it a *lust* for art. Such a person puts much of life aside, sometimes even daily sustenance to pursue art. But desire is not enough. Many people desire to be artists yet fail—but not because they lack talent. Talent, according to Hegel, means the skill to work with a medium: words, paint, wood, light, and such. Still, desire and talent are not enough. The artist must also have an unusual imagination, and this imagination often makes the artist different from other people in appearance and behavior.

But even imagination is not enough. Great art, good art, is only made by a person who also possesses *genius*. Genius is that rare ability to synthesize reason and emotion in a way that expresses the spirit (*Geist*) of the age. Therefore, people who study history often delve deep into the art of each epoch. Yet, genius is a gift that cannot be taught. As Shakespeare reminded us, "Some are born great, some achieve greatness, and some have greatness thrust upon 'em."[32]

Regimes in the last few centuries built political institutions on the premise that the genius of Western art created a superior culture. Karl Popper provides a cautionary element to any investigation of Hegel's aesthetics.[33] Along with the misuse of Hegel, Plato's idealism and Aristotle's empiricism have also been distorted by religious and political leaders who reference them for political legitimacy. Instead of advocating nationalistic superiority, we need

31. Hegel, *Philosophy of Fine Art*, vol. I, 380–82.

32 Shakespeare, *Twelfth Night*, Bevington, 2.5.142–44.

33. "Georg Wilhelm Friedrich Hegel," *Stanford Encyclopedia of Philosophy.*

to consider more universal theories that cannot be limited by any epoch, culture, government, or religion. Whenever possible, theories of art should consider all cultural contributions in developing a more universal aesthetic. It sounds daunting, of course. Who can absorb that much information? But do not be discouraged; Hegel comforts all those who yearn for truth with this reminder: the eternal spirit is breaking into history to alter our lives. That is the function of art. The result is that the arts improve our perceptions, faith, relationships, and life conditions.

The post-Hegelians often addressed one of Hegel's main points, the material foundation of his dialectic, and explored it to its maximum extent. They were influential in their time but today are seen as transitional figures. Tolstoy had a major impact on narrative writing, but his observations on art have not endured. He emphasized that artists express feelings directly through artwork and that viewers will be able to replicate the same feeling. It is like an infection that begins with the artist and then is transferred to all who witness the work.[34] Ideas about art are irrelevant because art cannot be reduced to thought. A work of art is an organism that is symbolic of life itself. Karl Marx (1818–83), on the other hand, focused on the material progression of society and how art, not just any art but artistic realism, can convey evidence of social progress. The distortions of Marxist thought by the former Soviet Union diminished his standing. Yet it is important to remember that his appeals to social and economic justice continue to have a hearing.[35] "From each according to their ability and to each according to their need"[36] has been a slogan for many liberation movements.

Another German, Friedrich Nietzsche (1844–1900), demonstrated a great affinity toward, and yet distance from, Hegel's aesthetics. Nietzsche's *Birth of Tragedy*[37] builds upon Hegel's dia-

34. Tolstoy, *What is Art?*, 40.

35. Harrington, *Art and Social Theory*, 124f.

36. "From each according to his ability, to each according to his needs" (*Jeder nach seinen Fähigkeiten, jedem nach seinen Bedürfnissen*) is a slogan popularized by Karl Marx in his 1875 *Critique of the Gotha Program*, Part I.

37. Nietzsche, *The Birth of Tragedy*, 19–21.

lectical method while making a complete U-turn away from it. He is not interested in how art reveals the transcendent but in how the arts resolve a strictly human struggle. For Nietzsche, the world is a nasty place filled with chaos. The thesis for Nietzsche is Apollonian rationalism, and the antithesis is Dionysian intoxication. These two forces, reason and ecstasy, are in a death struggle in which both attempt to annihilate the other. In the end, reason and emotion are rescued by artistic expression, especially music, which forms a synthesis redeeming not just human life but the universe itself. Art is the only hope for humanity because without it the human community would descend into continual and utter chaos. Such a state of affairs would be not just the end of history but the death of humanity. In this way, art rescues not just the individual or community but history itself from a self-destructive course. Art alone has the power to intervene in this struggle because the transcendent spirit is absent and without a voice. Nietzsche, declared with some gusto that "God is dead: of his pity for man hath God died."[38] Zarathustra declares that the God of the Western tradition, the lofty and serene God of Plato's eternal idea, is no longer. Civilization now depends on employing the arts to establish justice since any divine intervention will not redeem the human condition.

The impact of Nietzsche on aesthetics and religion is still churning in kettles of philosophical debate. Ancient Greek tragedy emerges anew from the Teutonic fires he lit under a cauldron. According to Nietzsche, only with the return to the ancient origins of the art form will modern civilization be rescued. Otherwise, we will destroy ourselves in our struggle between the rationality of Apollo and the ecstasies of Dionysus. Those two forces are headed toward mutual destruction, and only the arts can transform them. Humans are the same way. We must employ the arts in our struggle to redeem ourselves because hope in divine intervention is a misplaced hope. That god, the *deus ex machina*, does not exist.

In the remainder of this discussion, I will consider recent voices in aesthetics who examine human experience as the basis for creating and responding to art. For many of them, following

---

38. *Thus Spake Zarathustra*, LX, Fourth Part.

Nietzsche, the struggle between reason and emotion is at the center of their thought.

2

A Century of Progress

Major writers who addressed a variety of approaches to aesthetics emerged in the twentieth century. Instead of developing a unified system for art theory, these scholars advanced diversity as the touchstone for new scholarship. Susanne K. Langer (1895–1985)[1] explored artistic expressiveness as a form of cognitive reasoning. In Chicago, John Dewey (1859–1952)[2] developed a pragmatic approach that explored learning theory and aesthetics, while another Chicagoan, George Dickie (1926–2020),[3] proposed an institutional and sociological theory for evaluating the quality of artworks. Martin Heidegger (1889–1976)[4] investigated the role of the artist as the creator of a new epistemology—art creates knowing. The Nobel Prize-winning playwright Wole Soyinka (1934–)[5] penned a political aesthetic that addresses art and justice. Arthur Danto (1924–2013)[6] pondered the end of art and transfiguration. Not only do his insights close the book on Kant and Hegel, but they

1. Langer, *Feeling and Form* and *Philosophy in a New Key*.
2. Dewey, *Art as Experience*, 231.
3. Dickie, *Evaluating Art*.
4. Heidegger, *Poetry, Language, and Thought*.
5. Soyinka, *Art, Dialogue, & Outrage*.
6. Danto, *The Transfiguration of the Commonplace*.

also suggest a new direction for aesthetic discourse. Theologian Douglas Adams (1945–2007) analyzed the material constructions of artists and explored how they reference transcendence. Finally, Maxine Greene (1917–2014), the most eclectic scholar of the arts in this group, advanced the bold thesis that the arts are the very glue that holds society together. In small or large ways, each author considers justice as a component of aesthetics.

Susanne K. Langer

Susanne K. Langer (1895–1985) boldly asserted that rational thought originates in the realm of feeling. "I am scouting the possibility that rationality arises as an elaboration of feeling."[7] That elaboration of feeling, in her analysis, resides in the expressive quality of art. She divides expressiveness into discursive and nondiscursive categories and identifies the nondiscursive as the most significant. Nondiscursive expression is capable of conveying feelings directly without the linear structure of language. The arts, for her, are like a window that allows feelings to be perceived directly by the audience. Expressiveness has its own logical structure by giving form to feeling. The arts provide the grammar (morphology) of feeling and have their own inner logic.[8] All art forms possess an inherent structure, even those forms that appear to dismantle thought structures. The modern musicians who compose atonal works, who stand in opposition to the Romantics, are creating their own language of expressiveness.

The arts give voice to larger cultural traditions and contexts. But do not be mistaken; feelings come first, and our rational thoughts are constructed from feelings. Consider this example. How many people decide to marry someone because they make a list of attributes, then measure each prospect they meet to see how many items on the list this candidate fulfills? Isn't that more logical than following one's feelings? Aren't feelings fickle, and logic, well

7. Langer, *Problems of Art*, 124.
8. Langer, *Philosophy in a New Key*, 238.

. . . logical? Or consider this: how many times do you choose from a menu because you logically know that kale is healthier for you than bacon? You may know that, but does that always rule your taste buds? Langer argues that we make logical decisions based on feelings. Even more importantly, we learn to trust new thoughts because they *feel* right. As the saying goes, "When in doubt, go with your gut."

If you assume that a life of feeling is living with chaos, think again. According to Langer, our feelings have an inner logic. They have their own syntax, which is more dependable than discursive thinking. The arts teach us how feelings feel. We begin to trust the structure of our feelings when we realize they provide valuable information. If two actors on stage stand far apart and yell at each other, that might seem comical. But should they stand face to face with fists in motion, we feel something quite different. Those feelings inform us, but because it is a play, we stay in our seats.

For Langer, this is a crucial idea: we learn to know our own feelings because the arts have taught us how feelings feel, and they connect life experience with thought. We can think rationally about our experiences because we are guided by our feelings.[9] Rational thought, even empirical observation, arises from feeling. To state it as clearly as possible: not all feelings can be expressed verbally, but all that is expressed verbally can be felt.

At a basic level, Langer provides another synthesis of the contrasting views of Plato's idealism and Aristotle's empiricism. Her approach is the opposite of both the ancients, who assumed that ideas and empirical observations guide our feelings. Catharsis, according to Langer, occurs when there is a unity of thought, feeling, and the structure of the artistic work. The structure is, in one sense, a Platonic idea, while the expressiveness of art is substantiated by genuine experience, hence Aristotle's empiricism. Both become essential for Langer's view of catharsis as the reorienting of our feelings and ideas. Art changes things because art is more than an object and more than a feeling. Rather, it is how we structure our

9. Langer, *Philosophy in a New Key*, 216.

feelings and knowledge.[10] It is the art symbol that integrates emotion and idea, which changes how we understand and feel. Arts, therefore, are not just a synthesis of this dichotomy but result in catharsis and wholeness.[11]

Langer's distinction between discursive and nondiscursive logic follows indirectly in the footsteps of Immanuel Kant, who contrasted scientific and aesthetic truth. For Langer, all that is felt that cannot be said is nondiscursive logic.[12] And since our thoughts emerge from our feelings, much of what is experienced cannot be expressed discursively. There is no need to struggle with language to explain a musical score, as the music itself is the best vehicle to communicate feelings. It is possible to describe the arts discursively, but the audience should always be cognizant of the reality that descriptions are never the same as becoming aware of the feeling expressed in a work. Words are a mediating device between the art and the listener. The performance will directly express the emotional depth of an artwork.

Many years ago, I walked with my father through the Sheldon Gallery on the University of Nebraska campus. I thought he would appreciate the paintings of landscapes, flowers, and animals. But they hardly drew his attention. Then, as we neared the end of our stroll, he stopped in front of a large reddish-orange painting by Mark Rothko. He was silent for some time and then finally stated with enthusiasm, "Now that is something, isn't it!" No words were needed; the fact that he stopped and stared quietly for so long was already evidence that this work tugged at his being. The colors expressed a feeling so powerfully that he needed to stop and pay attention. During those quiet moments, he was dwelling on the expressiveness of that work. It was more powerful than the pretty paintings he had passed by with an air of indifference.

The art symbol is Langer's most debated idea, which explains why she returned to it repeatedly. The art symbol stands in contrast with symbols (e.g., stars, rainbows) in art, which do not interest

10. Langer, *Problems of Art*, 124.
11. Langer, *Philosophy in a New Key*, 215.
12. Langer, *Philosophy in a New Key*, 79ff.

her. The symbol in art is, as many theologians assume, something material that is intended to reference something transcendent.[13] The art symbol, by contrast, expresses emotions, complex relationships, similarities, and differences.[14] The art symbol emerges from a tangle of human experiences that is so laden with emotion that it can be best expressed through art and not with language. Discourse tends to present thoughts in a linear form, whereas the art symbol confronts the audience directly with feelings. Those feelings are the origin of new thoughts. The art symbol is material (music score, play text, painting) that is also given expressive form via artistic expression (piano, performers, canvas). Material is essential because it is the foundation for constructing a work, but it must express more than the material itself. The art symbol is a structured feeling that emerges from unstructured emotions. What Langer means at this level is that we all have feelings that are unstructured, although not chaotic,[15] and those unstructured feelings are given shape and order by means of art. Finally, those nondiscursive feelings give rise to words, knowledge, and contemplation. The artist works on all three levels: awareness of unstructured feelings, learning the shape of those feelings (anger, love, envy), and then expressing them via the art symbol. The artist is the creator of art symbols that, through their expressive power, structure the feelings of the audience and thus provide catharsis. And when that is repeated, over time and in other spaces, art creates a cultural heritage.[16] The art symbol relies on heritage, or heritages, as a guide to new expressive forms, which then shape new reflection and thought. The artist can lead others to become aware of that sequence, which would be an aid to all of humanity. Feelings are not suppressed or denied but are, in fact, building blocks of civilization.

13. Tillich, *Systematic Theology*, vol. 2, 10.
14. Langer, *Feeling and Form*, 51.
15. Langer, *Problems of Art*, 139.
16. Langer, *Feeling and Form*, 410.

John Dewey

John Dewey (1859–1952)[17] approached aesthetics with a pragmatic view. The artist creates the work, and the work creates an effect on an audience that must create a response to gain meaning from the experience. Each step requires the expression of feeling. The artist begins with a feeling and gives shape to it. The work must be expressive of feeling for the audience to connect with it. That connection results in the audience creating an expressive response.

Expressiveness to Dewey means feelings that might be unformed, chaotic, or even confusing. An intelligent artist takes those feelings and molds them into forms that we recognize as music, sculpture, or dance. If a person rages in the street or screams on stage, they are releasing emotions but not creating art. Those unfocused emotions are the opposite of art: they may be incomprehensible and alienating. The goal of the artist is to create a work that will be expressive in its own way. It is not the artist's expressiveness that the recipient perceives but the expressiveness inherent in the artwork. By viewing the central character in *Hamlet*, we will experience his emotional and intellectual struggle, but what we cannot do is know the feelings Shakespeare had as he was writing the play. The same is true for all works of art. It is the audience that encounters the work and is impacted by its expressiveness. And the audience has the responsibility to create meaning from that encounter.

This process from artist to work to recipient illustrates the artistic experience. Each step needs to be seen as expressive. Freedom of expression is at the heart of the triad. The artist must have freedom to create, the work of art must be free from encumbrances, and the viewer must be free to experience the expressiveness of the work. Freedom is not limited to political or religious freedom. Freedom means the ability to discover emotions in oneself and the ability to give them form. The freedom to exhibit those forms must come without political or religious meddling. Each person will need the freedom to respond in a meaningful way to the work.

17. Dewey, *Art as Experience*, chapters 2–5.

After a work is created, the artist's effort is complete. From that point onward, the artist must grant freedom for the recipient to respond in their own way.

The Russian playwright Anton Chekhov (1860–1904) provides an excellent example of a variety of responses to an auditory event. This dialogue from *The Cherry Orchard* (1903) illustrates how diverse humans are even in commonplace situations:

> (*They all sit deep in thought. . . . Suddenly, a distant sound is heard, coming out of the sky, like the sound of a string snapping*)
>
> Liubov: What was that?
>
> Lopakhin: I don't know. Somewhere a long way off, a lift cable in one of the mines must have broken. But it must be somewhere very far away.
>
> Gayev: or perhaps it was some bird . . . a heron, perhaps.
>
> Trofimov: Or an owl . . .
>
> Liubov: (*Shudders*). It sounded unpleasant, somehow . . .
>
> Feers: It was the same before the misfortune: the owl hooted, and the samovar kept singing.[18]

The twang they heard was not even a song or a chord. Yet that minimal sound evokes a variety of responses, which are recorded not just because they vary so much but because each character hears it according to their own life experience. No one agrees about what they heard. Each character is permitted the integrity of their response. Chekhov does not guide us as to which is the correct or even the best reaction. There is freedom in the dialogue and yet deep bonding in that moment.

Art builds relationships on micro and macro levels. Art liberates people from isolation and alienation by creating meaningful experiences that link the creator and the recipient. Those links are vital for society to function. Art invites each person to engage others who also find meaning in similar artistic moments.

18. Chekhov, *Plays*, 365.

That all sounds serious, and of course, Dewey is a serious thinker. Yet he recognizes that for art to be meaningful, it must be integrated with life. If we confine artistic experiences to the gallery or the theatre, we have failed to engage art in a meaningful way. An artistic experience will shape our life choices after the artistic event. The art event does not have an ending per se but is often the beginning. After we have had a meaningful session with an etching of Rembrandt or a novel by one of the Brontë sisters, that encounter continues to shape our life in unpredictable ways. And it may not even be exceptional art that impacts people.

When I was in first grade in a small country school, I was the curtain puller at the annual Christmas program. I was diligent and conscientious with this assignment. No one in the room, including myself, could have predicted the lifelong impact that one event would have. The experience provided something hard to explain except that it transformed my self-awareness and, therefore, self-understanding. The feeling of being onstage with an important "performance duty" created an experience unlike anything else I had known until then. That experience led me to seek out similar opportunities. And I found them.

Art is accessible to all in society. There is art beyond museum walls, books, and journals. Art has value if people experience it and allow it to shape their daily lives. There are artistic approaches to life in many forms, which make access to art a democratic experience. But do not be mistaken; the artist is someone who knows best how to express emotions through form, and those forms, whether they be poems, novels, or paintings, are how we experience art in the most meaningful way. A table setting might be artistically done but is generally not done to give expressive form to feeling. In this manner, Dewey attempts to distinguish practical artistic forms from expressive artistic forms. But the lines can be blurry.

The weakness in this construct is that not all that is called art has expressive value. That means the artist did not give feelings an expressive form. Or maybe the work was not expressive for the viewers. There are times, of course when a work does not evoke pleasant feelings but does just the opposite: aggravate. But the artwork still has value even in those situations. Aggravation is also a strong feeling, and if a work can evoke that, it becomes our responsibility to interpret its meaning.

Art is unique because it is transitional. There is a noticeable before and after with many artistic experiences. The impact of a work of art on one's feelings does not end when the concert ends. That life beyond the experience is what Dewey calls the transitional effect. That effect continues beyond the initial experience and has a transforming impact. A transformation of self is an experience rooted in an aesthetic moment. When we dine out, the dinner ends. When we drive to a park, the arrival is the end of the drive. But the experience of a work of art does not have those endings. The experience of a work of art often leads to knowledge. And this is the key for Dewey: what we learn is ourselves in relation to others. That is the power of art. It teaches us to be aware of each other and recognize our common experiences.

The danger here is that knowledge can be like a pond with distinct boundaries that keep us from looking beyond the water's edge. Art is more like a river that flows from where it started to the place we are now, and it will continue into areas we have not seen. The river flows with twists and bends. An expressive work of art may do the same: cause course changes in our lives. When that occurs, it frees our imaginations to think in new ways. And more importantly, it frees our emotions to value social relationships. Because history is never static, it is important that we continue to learn over time. Art, for John Dewey, is the most reliable instrument for personal and social growth.

Martin Heidegger

Heidegger (1889–1976) established his credentials as a philosopher of note with the publication of *Being and Time* (*Sein und Zeit*) in 1926.[19] Initially, he never expressed any views on politics and

19. This paragraph is a summary of the details found in Steiner's *Martin Heidegger*, 120–24, and Arendt, *Letters 1925–1975*, 239.

did not get involved with any political movements. That changed in 1934 when the faculty at the University of Freiburg overwhelmingly elected him as their rector (president). He was their second choice after the initial candidate was rejected by the Berlin regime for being too liberal. In his inaugural address, he expressed his hope for a new Germany under the leadership of the National Socialist Party. One of his initial actions was to reject a purging of Jewish books from the University Library and another was to reject pressure from Berlin to support the student Nazi party. Six months after assuming the presidency, he abruptly resigned when the Berlin regime demanded that he dismiss two liberal professors who were critical of Hitler. After his resignation as rector in 1934, Heidegger left the National Socialist Party. Two years later, he issued an article titled "Essay on Humanism," which advised philosophers to avoid all political involvement or even make political applications of their views. It was a complete reversal from his inaugural address.

Then, he was silent and did not publish again until the fall of the Third Reich. But before the Berlin regime collapsed, he was dismissed from the University, handed a shovel, and assigned manual labor on the banks of the Rhine River. His decline was visible to all: from a position of great prestige, he was sent downhill into the muck along the Rhine. In 1952, he was reinstated as a professor at Freiburg. Steiner concludes this section with, "I have been unable to locate anti-Jewish sentiments or utterances by Heidegger, which isolates him from mainstream National Socialism."[20]

Two Jewish Scholars, Hannah Arendt (1906–75) and George Steiner (1929–2020), highlight those details as partial vindication of Heidegger's reputation as a philosopher of merit who was deluded, for a few months, by a diabolical regime. On the other side of the debate, Heidegger's philosophical rival Karl Jaspers held that Heidegger was an unreconstructed Nazi well into the postwar period. Even George Steiner acknowledges that Heidegger's postwar silence on the Holocaust cannot be explained other than by his adamant refusal to say anything about politics. The most

20. Steiner, *Martin Heidegger*, 124.

vocal American critic of Heidegger, Tom Rockmore, ends his four-hundred-page book with this observation: "Despite his undeniable philosophical capacities, Heidegger's thought is weakened by his evident failure to understand the world in which he lived."[21] Hans Sluga supports this idea by stating that in his initial involvement with National Socialism, Heidegger quickly became disillusioned and withdrew into a private world, which was quietly tolerated by the regime.[22] Sluga goes on to say, in his assessment of Heidegger's *Der Spiegel* interview of 1956, that Heidegger's "political engagement in 1933 had been mistaken," that he had become disillusioned with the political process and now believed only in the power of political thinking."[23] Hannah Arendt made an even more emphatic claim in her 1969 tribute to Heidegger. "Of course, Heidegger recognized this 'mistake' after a short time and risked considerably more than was common at German Universities."[24] His mistake was to fall into the trap of thinking that philosophy could intervene with history and improve the political situation.

His reputation is still marred by his brief infatuation with the ideals of National Socialism. Marred because, as Richard Wolin[25] points out, his philosophical system allows for the nature of that regime and continues to provide an intellectual foundation for nationalism and racial politics. It may seem like a paradox that he continues to provide insights and language for the philosophical agendas of both the left and the right. It is possible that his emphasis on being, difference, dwelling in, and identity are foundational for more than one avenue of thought. One of his final publications, *Poetry, Language, Thought*,[26] examines the arts. Philosophers need to avoid political engagement, he says, and reflect on the beingness, presence, and meaning in the arts.

21. Rockmore, *On Heidegger's Nazism and Philosophy*, 368.

22. Sluga, *Heidegger's Crises*, 252.

23. Sluga, *Heidegger's Crises*, 238.

24. Arendt, *Letters: 1925–1975*.

25. Wolin, *Heidegger in Ruins*.

26. The German publication was released in 1956 and the English translation became available in 1971. *Poetry, Language, Thought*.

Martin Heidegger's aesthetic was also a break from European idealism and empiricism.[27] In one sense, he began at the beginning, with the pre-Socratic philosophers, who questioned the nature of things that exist and how they function. With those basic questions, Heidegger begins by defining what art is by sorting out the connection between existence and essence. He states that art is that which an artist creates, and the artist is the one who creates art. That sounds simple, but it leaves out many possibilities. For example, a pleasing piece of driftwood on a beach is not art. Neither is a gorgeous sunset. But a painting of the sunset, even a contorted one, and many pieces of driftwood formed into a shape become art. The existence of art as a physical object is not the same as its essence because the essence is how that object is art and not just decoration or equipment. If you paint a wall, you relate to that wall as equipment (dividing you from the outside), but if you paint a portrait on that same wall, it takes on a new essence, which we call art.

His analysis emphasized the work of art and the work that art does. With that definition, Heidegger examines how art functions. Art reveals. Art authenticates. Heidegger uses the image of a "rift design" to describe how art discloses and conceals truth.[28] Since I associate the term "rift design" with earthquake fault lines, I will use the phrase "rift line" instead of rift design. Where are these rift lines, and what do they disclose? The universe is made of things that we know as substances. Some things emanate meaning to us. That can occur when we see iron and wood together because they might be more than just the material. Iron and wood, assembled by an artist in a planned construct, become a work of art. In the same way, a rift line is more than it appears. It reveals that there is something underneath, something more powerful than the rift line itself. We cannot see the tectonic plates, but we understand that they are there. Understanding a power that is not visible is what Heidegger calls comprehending the essence of a thing. For

27. Heidegger, *Poetry, Language, Thought,* 5ff. See the addendum for further discussion of the controversies surrounding Heidegger.

28. Heidegger, *Poetry, Language, Thought,* 63.

example, we may not see freedom, but we can see what freedom of the press does. We may not see dedication, but we can see meals being served, medical services being provided, and houses rebuilt after a storm. They provide the material *essence* of a power we comprehend but cannot see.

Rift lines are evidence that beneath the surface of the earth, tectonic plates rub against each other, which can cause quakes, which in turn leave these lines. The lines are not quakes, and they are not the plates. But those lines disclose where plates are and their potential force. Rift lines draw our attention because of the disruption and destruction they reveal. Wherever there are strong rift lines, human life can be precarious. But like icebergs, it is not the rift line that is dangerous; it merely discloses the dangers that lurk beneath the surface. The dangerous forces remain hidden, but no one should ignore them because they are powerful and unpredictable. Art functions in much the same way. It is made of substances; it is a thing, and simultaneously, it is more than its own thingness. We experience its essence as a play, a dance, or a painting. We can observe substances, but when presented with essences, we dwell in them—they occupy and take on a new existence in our imagination.

Art reveals a rift line. It is a marker that discloses the location of tectonic plates that clash in society, individuals, or institutions. That revelation can often be disturbing, not because art itself is troubling but because audiences know that it marks the place where calamities have occurred and will likely occur again. The material, the work of art, should not be rejected or belittled because to do so only hides the dangers that lurk along the divisions revealed by the rift lines. Instead, Heidegger suggests that we dwell on those dividing lines to understand why these misfortunes recur. It is apparent that with his emphasis on disclosure, Heidegger walks in the footsteps of Aquinas, who emphasized that the arts bring clarity to the human experience.

Rift lines that have historically caused considerable harm include religious differences, racial demarcations, gender issues, and political calamities. Everyone should ask: to what degree do we dwell on those lines of difference to understand their essence? That process has the power to transform us so that we can prepare ourselves and not fear any future clashes on a tectonic scale. In this way, art reveals what is concealed. Art is truth disclosing itself to us and showing us the true nature of existence.

The act of revealing is illustrated by Vincent van Gogh's *A Pair of Shoes* (1886), one of several paintings of peasant shoes he made during his lifetime. This is a close-up, dark painting of a woman's black shoes. They are very worn from arduous work and seem suspended with a light circling around them. Is this a halo effect? The painting is about equipment but, at the same time, more than that. If a viewer dwells on that material image, eventually, the essence, the truth, will be disclosed. And what is disclosed? Remember, essence is what emanates from the material; it's not a substance. What is revealed, according to Heidegger, is the life of a woman who has led an existence of hard, physical labor.[29] She is poor, and her work consists of digging potatoes. The shoes indicate she has endured dirt, mud, and rain, and she has a hard time paying her bills. We can tell because these shoes are old, they are past due, one might say. By dwelling on the painting and grasping its essence, the viewer is transformed. We see shoes, but the subject of the painting is not in the painting (just as the tectonic plates are not seen, but the fault line gives evidence of their power and existence). To understand the woman is to understand the other who exists. That is the work that art does: it discloses the truth of our existence, which is often hidden, the truth that sets us free.

29. Heidegger, *Poetry, Language, Thought*, 32f.

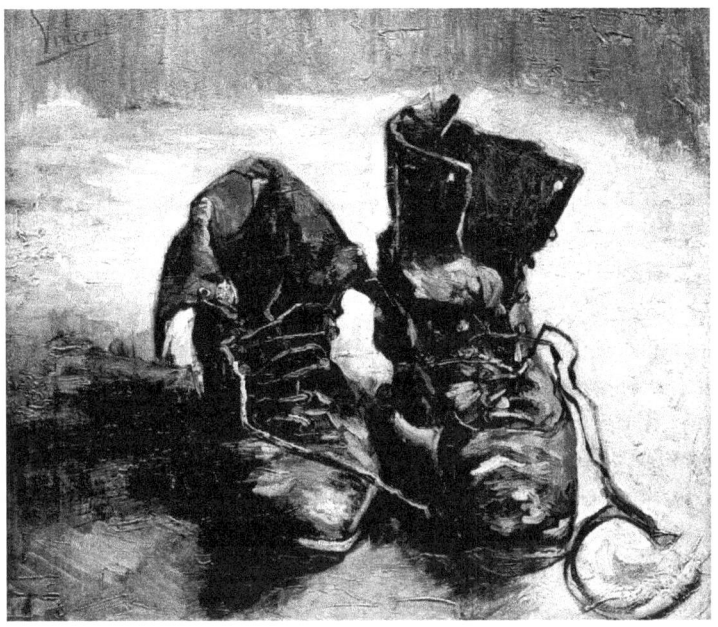

Art, for Heidegger, discloses to us the authentic being of things. Art is truth revealing itself to the world. This is not to say, in the manner of scientific rationalism, that art has logical meaning, nor does it merely stir up feelings, as many Romantics advocated. The revelations that art provides lead to an understanding of self and the authentic existence of others. Because of our need to understand the existence of others, art should be visited and revisited every day because "art transfigures the world in its existential interconnectedness."[30] In that way, art returns to its original function, which the Greeks understood as a spiritual experience that authenticates all beings, even the beingness of stone and wood. In the hands of an artist, marble is transfigured into a new being. We are made new by dwelling in the beingness of art. Interestingly, art does not need to be beautiful to reveal the truth, to make us aware of the rift lines, and that awareness opens the possibility of transfiguration.[31] The beauty lies in what is disclosed and not in the

30. Austin Harrington, *Art and Social Theory*, 178.

31. Heidegger, *Poetry, Language, Thought*, 36.

material or equipment of a work of art. Some artworks reveal the rift points more authentically than others, and with the passing of time, those works emerge with greater significance. This perspective is a word of caution about jumping to conclusions too quickly. Ben Jonson and not Shakespeare, for example, was the playwright Queen Elizabeth revered.

The artist's being, their identity, is their existence. Art is an expression of the artist's being. What art expresses is the essence of the work itself, and the work is an expression of the artist's essence. It is upon reflection on the essence of art that we understand the artist's identity and existence. The artist's existence is often on the fault line where disruptions occur. The crises of those fault lines become, in the hands of the artist, the essence of the work of art.

For Heidegger, there is no distinction between good and bad art. Art that discloses the truth of being is art, but works that fail to disclose the truth are not art. They are not bad art; they are not art at all. They may be beautiful. But the quality of beauty does not make them art, and they can be considered decoration. There is nothing wrong with wanting decoration and adornment, but that should not be confused with art, which discloses truth. Because in revealing existence, beingness, a work has existence as art. Equipment and decoration are alternatives to art. Tools, for example, are useful and fulfill our need for work. Decoration is needed to adorn the world and the things we build. A well-made tool is better than a badly made one, but neither exists as art. Equipment is made for its usefulness, and if it is old and no longer used, it can be used for decoration, such as antiques hung on walls. Such objects may serve to bring back memories, but seldom, if ever, do they disclose truths.

Because art is a being and because beings such as humans and animals change with time, does that mean that artworks change? Yes, according to Heidegger. Because no artwork worthy of being called art is ever the same when we revisit it, the paint does not change, but our awareness of it does. What it discloses a second time will be different from the first, and in that sense, it lives. It is a being. If someone says, "I love that song. It makes me feel the same way every time I hear it," we should be skeptical. Things that make us feel the same way every time might include a toothbrush, a chair, or a piece of toast. But if someone says that of a work of art, then it has probably ceased to be a living being for you, and it has become propaganda. That is harsh. But remember, Heidegger was drafting this book at the height of World War II when Nazi songs rallied the faithful to join demonstrations.

Art is a complicated matter. The fault lines on earth both reveal and conceal the power that created such a disruption to the earth's crust. Art simultaneously conceals and reveals to the audience the power that resides in the beingness of art. Works of art that demonstrate that paradox become works in which we can dwell and, therefore, will have greater meaning for us. In contrast, many works seldom, if ever, stop us in our tracks and ask us to dwell. This is the unique contribution of the artist who creates art: they have the power to reveal and conceal authentic beings.[32] Equipment (*techne*) does not reveal or conceal, and neither does reason or logic. Art is fundamental to comprehending authentic existence. It is so basic that with works of art, the world remakes itself by shaking up the old, former identities and settling again in a new way.[33]

George Dickie

George Dickie (1926–2020) was a professor of philosophy at the University of Illinois-Chicago. He formulated the institutional theory[34] of art, which he also called "art as social currency." In his view, the value of art is determined by art institutions, and an artist is someone who has been identified as such by art institutions. Art institutions include schools, magazines, museums, galleries, theatres, and book publishers. This seems typical of our time. A student is awarded an MFA in studio art and thereby recognized as

32. Steiner, *Martin Heidegger*, 134.
33. Heidegger, *Poetry, Language, and Thought*, 44.
34. Dickie, *Aesthetics: An Introduction.*

an artist. A poet is hired by a university's creative writing program to teach poetry and, from that day forward, is recognized as a poet. A poet is a poet if they have published in a literary magazine. If, on the other hand, the work is published by a local newspaper, that alone would not result in making you part of the art world. An actor who is never cast in a show is not an actor, no matter how entertaining they are at family reunions. When the Field Museum in Chicago put up a display of art painted by chimpanzees, that did not make the chimpanzee an artist. But if the Art Institute of Chicago put up the same display, then people would acknowledge that chimpanzees can be artists. A person can write plays that remain hidden in a drawer, and so is never recognized as a playwright. But if those plays are discovered a hundred years later, voilà! That person becomes a playwright posthumously. Such is the example of Georg Büchner. His unpublished plays were found in a desk drawer approximately forty-five years after his death. If a person writes a play that is staged, they are immediately hailed as a playwright. That is the way the art world works. We might criticize, make cynical jokes, or decide to join it. There are very few alternatives to those options.

Sounds easy, doesn't it? All I can say is, go ahead, try it. What Dickie understands is that the art world has procedures and standards that can be intimidating or even seem prohibitive. Even within each discipline, there are levels of acceptability or recognition. Plays are expressions of diversity even when we may not be conscious of that dimension. As critic Ruth Hamilton notes of actor Derek Jacobi's playing of the character Hamlet, "There are as many Hamlets as there are actors who play him. And nobody can be the definitive Hamlet because the definitive Hamlet doesn't exist."[35] Hamilton's insight coincides with Marvin Rosenberg's voluminous study of actors who played Hamlet.[36] Rosenberg goes into considerable detail to identify similarities and differences in character interpretation. He approaches the performers with a

---

35. Hamilton, "Derek Jacobi—Claudius Contemplates Hamlet."
36. Rosenberg, *The Masks of Hamlet.*

variety of research methods: live shows, film and television versions, videos, and interviews.

Due to the durability of the Bard from Stratford-upon-Avon and the pliability of his characters, contemporary playwrights have a major challenge. Shakespeare festivals abound around the globe, but seldom does another writer rise to Shakespeare's level of endurance. Today, a playwright might turn out script after script, but unless their plays are produced in New York City, Chicago, or Los Angeles, they will probably be turned down by every major script publishing house in the United States. Even a person with an MFA in playwriting often cannot find a theatre to produce their work.

Dickie acknowledges that within the art world, there is a hierarchy of values. If a person asks who the best playwright in English is, the answer must be Shakespeare. Why? Because his collected works rank number three in the world's most published works. Ahead of him is the number one seller, the Bible (all translations), and number two, the Quran. But even Shakespeare's impact is not worldwide. Wole Soyinka notes that in Africa, for example, he is not as dominant a playwright as in other parts of the globe.[37] Yet, for persons in theatre, we can be pleased that a playwright stands next to Mohammed and Jesus! No matter what one's religious affiliation is, we find it comforting to know that a playwright is so close to God.

Beauty is not a factor in evaluating art. Some art may be beautiful and fetch wide acclaim, but some might just as well be dreadful. But if the art world accepts a beautiful work and an atrocious work and sets them side by side, people usually begin to see the beauty of both. That is the power the art world has over the general public. Then, if one, or only one, gallery or museum decides to see value in such a work, soon, the work will find a permanent place in the art world. Human perceptions are that pliable and can easily be shaped by declarations from the art world! Can one disagree with this and, at the same time, acknowledge that this is how the art world works?

---

37. Soyinka, *Art, Dialogue, & Outrage*, 205.

The market forces in art become the standard for determining value, according to Dickie. A painting that sells for ten million dollars must be much better than one that sells for only one million! A bestseller on the *New York Times* list must be a much better book than an unlisted one written by a local historian or novelist. If a theatre in New York charges you $125 a ticket for Anton Chekhov's *The Cherry Orchard*, it is obvious it will be much better than a $50 ticket to a Chicago production of the same play. A good artist will know how to manage those market forces and adjust to them. Lesser artists will be baffled by, hostile to, or simply shut out from the art world. There are no other factors by which we can reliably determine the value of art. Or are there? Dickie has his critics. Some are direct, others more subtle.

Arthur Danto

Arthur Danto (1924–2013) was of the former, direct party. He came armed with heavy cannons to announce the "end of art," by which he meant the end of a tradition. The Western legacy, he suggested, had exhausted itself, and so had the West's philosophy of art. The artistic and philosophical links between the past and the present are now broken. Things had not reached a proverbial brick wall; instead, they developed to the point where nothing more could be added. The ending came not with a bang but a whimper. A lamp that had lit Western culture for millennia finally came to the end of its wick. However, Danto did not simply announce an end, he also proposed a new beginning. This would not be culture-bound by centuries of tradition, and it would provide a profound sense of freedom for the artist.

According to Danto, the West has experienced four phases in art history: (1) Before art, when artistic work served religious or secular purposes. (2) The age of art, which began in 1400 CE and ended in 1800. Art was created for its own sake—beauty, form, structure. (3) Art as a manifesto—proclamations regarding social, economic, and religious life from 1800–1970s. (4) The end of art occurred in the 1970s when art became play. In this ending phase, which was also a beginning, the artist plays with color, shape, reality, perception, and words to explore connections, relationships, and spontaneity.

Writing decades earlier than Danto, in 1938, Johan Huizinga noted that culture is developed by human play.[38] Not only does the artist play with the basic elements of art, but the work itself seems to be playful. It is about teasing the sense rather than making declarative claims. Play playfully transforms the material, and the artwork stimulates our senses. Those are the ingredients, Danto claims, of current art.

At one level, this view of art identifies art as "play" and nothing more. And yet, it is more. As Huizinga points out: (1) Play is more than play. It is how people organize themselves and develop knowledge that is above and separate from play. (2) Play acknowledges our participation, not just presence, in the human community. As individuals, it is through play that we become part of the whole. What Huizinga hints at (and Danto recognizes) is that art and play both go hand in hand as they transform our sense of being, and they bring pleasure in unexpected ways.[39] After all, isn't that what humans do with a cat? For both Danto and Huizinga, the play transforms and transfigures our reality.

This new interpretation of art—that it transfigures our reality—has parallels to the biblical transfiguration narrative.[40] The Synoptic Gospels (Matt 17:1–9; Mark 9:2–8; Luke 9:28–36) all record that when Jesus walked up a mountain with his disciples, they were startled by what they saw. Jesus's face suddenly glowed, and beside him stood Moses and Elijah, representing the law and the prophets. At that moment, this man became more than just another rabbi. Not only did he appear side by side with the icons of the Jewish religious tradition, but he also became the new voice of that tradition.

Danto claims that contemporary art functions in a manner similar to that of transfiguration. What happened to those religious

38. Huizinga, *Homo Ludens*.
39. Huizinga, *Homo Ludens*, 11.
40. Danto, *The Transfiguration of the Commonplace*, ii–iii.

figures and how they were seen in a new light also occurs in contemporary art. The commonplace is transfigured. Danto references Andy Warhol's *Brillo Box* (1964) to illustrate his view. Warhol's work is made of plywood and paint. The painted sculpture is not about religious heroes—not Moses, Elijah, or Jesus—and, in fact, it is a strange reproduction of packaging for a name-brand cleaning agent. A traditionalist might well ask: wasn't the biblical story a singular event about a religious figure? Yes, that was a singular religious event. But the process of having something ordinary and familiar transfigured due to the skill and insight of an artist is new. And in the process of observing the work of art, the viewer is also changed. Viewers may be startled by what they see, their ordinary day becoming something other than ordinary. Therefore, they also are transfigured by the commonplace. Art changes how we see things, even mundane elements such as plywood and paint. As T. S. Eliot noted, we can leave a place, circle the globe, and return where we started and see it for the first time.[41] That is why we do not cease exploration.

For a transfiguration to occur, the artist takes commonplace materials (plywood, paint) and changes them into something other than what they were before. What the artist makes may be startling in its realism or shocking in its departure from expectations. But in either case, a special aura of complexity, confusion, and awe surrounds a work. Remember: the artist is not the only "actor" in that narrative. The viewer who gazes at what has been transfigured will also be changed. Traditional rules and conventions, as well as the spirit (the prophetic) in art, are changed in such a way that the viewer is confronted with this new turn. A viewer who stops and takes note of this change may also be transfigured by the experience. When that occurs, the artwork will be seen in a new light, even if you do not believe in halos. That is how that term is used by Danto and in this essay.

The end of art is evident to Danto because narrative structures no longer have the emotional resonance that Aristotle claimed they should have. The function of art is no longer to experience

41. Eliot, *The Complete Poems and Plays*, 145.

catharsis. Healing is not a goal when illumination will do. Kant's multiplicity of aesthetic experience is, according to Danto, more psychology than art. Synthesis is no longer desirable in art, so Hegel has been tossed aside, and who today cares about Nietzsche's abyss? These voices were great in the past, but we have absorbed their meaning and moved on, so they no longer describe the art of our age. Also, when Dickie writes about the art world, he shows his age. There is no art world anymore. Today's prophets are painting on subway walls, as Paul Simon noted, so who then needs a gallery?[42] And as to Langer, it saddens Danto to say that emotional reactions to art are also a phenomenon of the past. The arts no longer disclose a convincing nondiscursive logic.

Sculpture today illustrates Danto's point. He has in mind a prominent bronze cat in a guest house in New York. It is a cat, but not a realistic one. It is larger than life and appears to have no fur. You do not see its hide or ribs. The sides are composed of nearly straight lines of metal. When Danto walks by this cat, which is chained to a newel post, it never evokes any feeling, positive or negative. It is there, and so is the newel post, which is useful, but the cat is not. It is not just nonfunctional; it is anti-functional. It neither pleases nor displeases. It is a sculpture intended to be art, so everyone calls it art. But it does not disclose a rift line or past calamities that would have come when the earth quaked.

And yet, Danto claims, it is more than brass and more than a meaningless shape. It shows better technique than many other works, so with its existence, it exudes an essence. It is a cat! No one would take it for a dog, a goat, or a coyote. In that sense, the act of recognition is pleasing not because of its beauty but because it has an observable identity. Danto implies, isn't that what we all strive for, the recognition of our identity? No one desires to be invisible, as Ralph Ellison so emphatically demonstrated in his great novel, *Invisible Man*.[43] There are times when to observe and be observed is pleasing. And that is what art, now at the end of a long artistic

---

42. "Banksy," *Encyclopedia Britannica*.
43. Ellison, *Invisible Man*.

tradition, can provide to those who desire to engage in artistic activity.

Danto's notion of the end of art also describes a trend in theatre. In 1955, Samuel Beckett's *Waiting for Godot* premiered in London. Viewers immediately sensed the unique character of this work. The first significant analysis was Martin Esslin's book, *The Theatre of the Absurd* (1961). His assessment of the play centered on the "static situation" in which the act of waiting becomes "absurd."[44] It is absurd because Beckett has upended centuries of theatre conventions and, at the same time, presented a new direction. I will address the conventions first.

Aristotle's *Poetics* introduced three essential components of a good play. The play should be set in one location (preferably in front of a temple), have one action that moves the plot forward, and should occur in one day, from sunrise to sunset. Aristotle, observing that in his play about Oedipus, Sophocles followed these "unities," recommended that all plays would benefit by doing likewise. Eventually, by the 1700s, many plays adhered slavishly to Aristotle's conventions. The French play *El Cid* (1636) serves as a prime example. In one day, the Moors invaded Spain, were driven back, reinvade, and finally, were driven out completely by Spanish forces led on horseback by the Spanish commander, El Cid—tied to his saddle because he was dead.

Beckett dismantled Aristotelian formalism. *Waiting for Godot* is set in a bog, and the principal characters, Vladimir and Estragon, remain unchanged from page to page. There is no passing of time. No one knows one day from the next. Vladimir and Estragon meet a messenger at the end of Act I who says, "Godot will come tomorrow." And he repeats that line at the end of Act II, but Godot never comes. The characters do not know what day it is, and neither do we.

This departure from the conventions of theatre created a clean break from tradition. This raw and direct encounter with nothingness releases the audience from expecting a normal plot, typical characters, and time markers to indicate the year, month, day, or

44. Esslin, *The Theatre of the Absurd*, 22.

hour. In a play where all normal expectations are abandoned, we end up with ourselves and our identities because the rest of the world has been, for all practical purposes, bracketed out. At the same time, the banter between these two vagabonds is captivating.

Beckett has created a new world, a world in which the characters and the audience dwell together. When a play does not follow the traditional conventions, the audience is presented with a world they do not recognize. They have a choice: enter that world with its mysteries or withdraw and not pay attention. In most cases, the audience is absorbed by the world of the play. In those moments, the audience experiences "the mystery of the arts in their capacity to invite us into another world to be enlivened and transformed."[45] In those moments, the production has a life of its own, for which the technical term is *ontology*. Mysteriously, a work of art made of materials (words, movement, wood, and canvas) can disclose an immaterial world that does not exist anywhere else. As Danto reminds us, never underestimate the transfiguration and the new awareness it reveals.

The nothingness and alienation described by existentialist philosophers are experienced on a visceral level in Beckett's staged works. Critic Hugh Kenner describes the audience: "We . . . clutch at straws of meaning, persuaded at the bottom of only one thing that all four men exist embodied, gravid, speaking: moving before us, their shadows cast on the wall."[46] Becket has stripped the play of all theatrical conventions by creating the most theatrically haunting play ever written. He creates the time, space, and narrative where that world becomes alive. And, paradoxically, the realm of nothingness creates another reality in the imagination of those who fully encounter the performance: a world beyond the stage. When we are absorbed by the world of the play, we are at the same time lifted beyond it.

With Heidegger in mind, it is one short step to realize that the bog is no place, the characters show no action, and their waiting is evidence that time does not pass. The question then is, what

---

45. Friesen, *Artists, Citizens, Philosophers*, 203.
46. Kenner, "Life in the Box," 111.

does this rift line disclose? What is revealed? The first reality is that the play creates its own being. As odd as it may seem, it has a life of its own. In philosophy, that is called ontology—the reality of existence. The play discloses how closely the existence of these characters mirrors our own existence. The characters show us our own loss of direction, purpose, and meaning as we also wait for a sign, a message, or anything that can intervene in our descent into meaninglessness.

Those who have been in the play or witnessed a production often recall entering an unknown realm and, because its impact lingers, experiencing the sensation of never being released from it. The ordinary things in life—the bog, the carrot, the tree, two hobos along a ditch somewhere—have an existence long after the curtain falls. The fault line, in this case, discloses a realm that goes deeply into awareness of self in a new way. Life is transfigured: what was commonplace is now set apart as a unique encounter with existence stripped of pretense.

Personal testimony has its limits, but this is relevant. As a freshman in college, I was in a production of *Waiting for Godot,* and my parents saw it. The next day, all they said was, "That was interesting." Many decades later, the day after my father's funeral, my mother spoke: "Dad and I talked about that play you were in, and we felt so lucky that our lives had more meaning." Even though they saw many of my plays, I knew which one she meant. Recently, people who saw that production more than sixty years ago commented on it as a memorable evening in the theatre. Plays can live long past their life on the stage. Plays have their own being and often continue to exist by creating indelible memories. Was it catharsis? On one level, yes: the audience gathered meaning and, therefore, consolation from it. They understood that art reveals the truth of being.

Douglas Adams

Douglas Adams (1945–2007) taught religious dance and visual arts at the Pacific School of Religion in Berkeley, California. His approach was to examine how contemporary artists reference religion and create religious experiences. Furthermore, his interests focused on artists who are opaque in how they express religion in their works, and he was not interested in the obvious, transparently religious work. No Sallman *Head of Christ* for him![47] His book *Transcendence with the Human Body in Art* (1991) examined George Segal, Stephen De Staebler, Jasper Johns, and Christo. His class lectures also relied heavily on Mark Rothko. Toward the end of his life, he stated that he viewed Rembrandt as the definitive painter who expressed religious awareness. Adams argued that the artist reveals to us a religious dimension not found in any other human endeavor. Therefore, it is imperative that we heed the work of the artist if we wish to call ourselves religious.

Adams pays careful attention to the work of the artist, and his analysis focuses on the ways in which that awareness is conveyed to the attentive viewer. George Segal's sculpture, *The Holocaust*, consists of plaster casts of victims in various stages of suffering and death in a concentration camp. Anyone who has seen photos of the Nazi death camps will recognize these figures. Segal places them behind barbed wire. The permanent exhibit is outdoors, at the Legion of Honor of San Francisco, off to the side of the parking lot and behind a retaining wall. It is not visible to the casual visitor; one must seek the work to find it. Already, there is a religious motif: those who seek truth will find it. But the arrangement of the bodies creates a modified crucifixion, and two of the bodies are of the biblical Abraham and Isaac. Isaac's hands are bound, and Abraham is holding his head. The voice of God does not intervene. A ram does not appear in the thicket.

None of this is obvious initially. But the viewer begins to sense a design to the arrangement and then begins to analyze. A careful observer notices that the sculpture is set in our world and simultaneously in the biblical world. That awareness connects the two worlds across the millennia. And it is then, often, that the bodies of Adam and Eve come into focus. In that one sculpture, the beginning and end of humanity are on full display. Contemplation

47. A 1940 portrait of Jesus by Warner Sallman.

of the Holocaust guides us to awareness of what transcends time, space, cultures, languages, and nation-states. It may even provoke awareness of the alpha and omega.

In considering Christo (1935–2020), Adams turned to his unique specialty: finding religious significance in works that seemingly carry no religious references. Christo is known for his monumental work. He used fabric to wrap the Berlin Reichstag, a museum in Bern, the Arc de Triomphe in Paris, and other well-known buildings. In Marin County, California, immediately north of San Francisco, he proposed a twenty-six-mile fence made of fabric. The resulting installation, *Running Fence* (1976), was not just fabric. Christo installed posts and cross beams to hold the cloth. The proposed object would traverse farmland, pass through small towns, and go over the low hills of that area. If you have ever planned anything that involved structures crossing many properties, you might imagine the complexity of this project. The hard part was not the material installation.

The difficulties came in surveying the most appropriate route and finding ways to negotiate with landowners, obtain code variances, and build community support to avoid sabotage or vandalism. The most appropriate route, for Christo, was not the way the crow flies—the shortest distance between two points. The most appropriate would be the most aesthetically pleasing. Only Christo would be able to devise that route based solely on his own visual assessment of the terrain. The challenge for Christo was not to establish unity but community. These two are not naturally opposed, but religious groups tend to divide themselves into those who seek doctrinal unity at the risk of breaking community versus those who seek community and will risk yielding principles of doctrine. Christo's challenge was to work toward community while being sensitive to unity.

Christo, in effect, proposed taking a two-dimensional landscape painting and transforming it into a three-dimensional work. Instead of making a small sculpture or maquette for a gallery, he aimed to physically place the work in the hills and fields of Marin County itself. Galleries are accustomed to patrons who connect or disconnect with their exhibits. But those are private transactions, and if audible, spoken in hushed tones. *Running Fence* breaks those conventions. People engage in dialogue, sometimes heated, long before the materials for the sculpture are ordered. *Running Fence* became a multiyear project that proceeded with starts, stops, and advances. As neighbors studied the plans, discussed matters with each other, hired lawyers to determine rights and liabilities, and worried about grazing problems in the pastures, opposition slowly withered. As people considered this thing no one had ever dreamed of before, they changed. One by one, they were transformed.

That was Christo's procedure. One farmer and then the next. One village permit and then the next. One ordinance variance and then the next. There was vocal and, at times, strong opposition at first, but by the time an association came together to form a community of *Running Fence* people, opposition had faded. Anxiety or hostility was there, and then it was gone. Eventually, the fence was built by neighbors who now relished their newfound appreciation for art! The neighborhood was changed. It was transformed.

After the structure was complete, the twenty-six-mile *Running Fence* became the pride of the neighborhood. People arrived from the surrounding area to walk its length. They visited in small and large groups. Those who had initially expressed vocal opposition became the best greeters and hosts for those who were curious to experience *Running Fence*. Even though the fence was hardly a religious object and contained no hidden religious symbols, it held uncanny religious significance: it built a community in a way nothing else could. And community, Adams emphasized, is absent in our schedule-driven, clock-obsessed world. If art can build a new sense of community among strangers, there is hope for the world. For some, it might be a glimpse of transcendence, but for many, it became a reality rooted in the way art builds community where it did not exist, at least at the same level. That, Adams claims, is transcendence through bodily experience. The fence encouraged people to walk, walk its length, have picnics along the way, and build stronger ties with friends and neighbors. From the stuff of earth, wood, and canvas, awareness rises. In the words of Paul

Tillich, "Every artistic expression is religious in the larger sense of religion."[48] Although Adams was a theologian and not a philosopher, his contribution is worth considering.

Maxine Greene

Maxine Greene (1917–2014) is the most eclectic of the people examined in this chapter. She references visual arts, literary arts, cinema, dance, music, theatre, and philosophy. She asserts a central role for the arts in education because they prepare people for life's challenges. Democracy, religion, and all the institutions of society are dependent upon the arts for their effectiveness.

Because the arts are foundational for learning, Greene emphasizes the need to be free to feel, to play, and to discover. The arts integrate those three elements, which form the foundation for knowledge. Feelings are the beginning point for her. Awareness of our emotions is vital to understanding ourselves and others. Our feelings are engaged when we play. Play is serious business. A person who loves playing with color and paint may develop into an artist. Another who loves playing with words might become a poet. For the person who enjoys playing with building blocks, architecture may one day beckon. The journey from playing to becoming skilled in an area involves discovery. But the discovery does not happen unless the journey begins. And a journey requires preparation. If we do not understand or have a sense of affinity for a work of art, we should not blame the artwork or artist. It is possible that we are not prepared for the journey that work requires of us. At each stage in that process, the learner will need a sense of freedom to connect feelings with the object that is created.

Greene says that because the arts function on so many levels in society, it is almost impossible to find any place in life where art is absent. She points out that people approach situations, each other, facts, and even the unknown with imaginations that seek beauty. For some, the discovery of new facts is beautiful, and

48. Tillich, *On Art and Architecture*, 33.

for others, beauty is a new idea or a relationship.[49] The aesthetic mind is continually preparing us to encounter the unknown and to gain meaning from it. Her wide-angle lens also enables her to focus on many specifics. We will now look at a few as they relate to aesthetics.

Greene builds her aesthetic theory on the principle of expressiveness. The work of art is expressive; our response will often be expressive, and future reflection on the work will encourage continued expressiveness.[50] This happens because we have the human capacity for aesthetic experiences and the ability to learn from them. There are instances when we feel deeply about an artistic encounter and recall that impact later. That happens because the artist has given us the freedom to respond in our own way. The artist does not dictate what we are supposed to feel but challenges us to feel and think. Many people react with strong feelings to Vincent van Gogh's painting, *The Starry Night* (1889). Many also react intensely to Carl Andre's *Equivalent VIII* (1966). Those responses, Greene says, guide us toward a better understanding of the world and ourselves. Liking or disliking might be the last comment we make about either work, but it should not be the first.

The arts are an expression of freedom and can only exist in a meaningful way in a free society. Democracy itself is dependent on artists to retain a political system where freedom thrives. Freedom includes the capacity to look at something that is and imagine it to be otherwise. The artist can help us look at a block of wood and see a sculpture that resides inside. The artist transforms material, and we are transformed by the result. Even though many ways of knowing are similar, the fact remains that the artist provides the means to imagine the future. The most basic thing the arts teach us is that individuals, even those with a different language and culture, can express meaningful ideas and feelings via the arts. One thing we owe people, especially those from other cultures, is to try to understand them.[51] That requires relationships based on a

---

49. Greene, *Variations on a Blue Guitar*, 21.

50. Greene, *Variations on a Blue Guitar*, 11f.

51. Greene, *Variations on a Blue Guitar*, 184.

willingness to journey, figuratively, into the unknown. And it is the artist who can guide us there.

Whenever we encounter a work of art, our human tendency is to find value in it or to dismiss it as unfitting. Greene emphasizes that we find meaning so that we will not dismiss works of art, even those we perceive as difficult or confusing. The arts express feelings and enable us to hold onto them. They become ideas and grow. The arts have a life of their own, and when we encounter them, we grow. That is the case, according to Greene, because art is the primary way we learn to know our own feelings and thereby understand the feelings others are experiencing. Those experiences change us, change our view of the other person, and, by extension, change society.[52]

The function of the arts in our personal lives and in society is to guide us through life. They can achieve that because the arts present us with aesthetic experiences: those beautiful moments that become markers in our lives. When we share an aesthetic experience with others, it has the potential to build a more cohesive group and society. And for that to occur, arts education is needed. Arts education is more than teaching skills. It necessarily involves teaching others how to encounter an aesthetic experience. In that way, we discover that what seemed impossible becomes possible. Everyone who has aesthetic experiences recognizes the human spirit is filled with untapped potential.[53] That reservoir residing in each of us as a great unknown can become known.[54] The artist and the art continue to disclose that truth.

The spirit of humanism dominates the writings of Greene with one variation that I will mention later. It is apparent to any reader that she advocates the exploration of human experience and identity and follows the implications of those discoveries.[55] The arts are central to that exploration, although what is garnered from such a quest reaches beyond the arts and becomes part of our

52. Greene, *Variations on a Blue Guitar,* 195.

53. Greene, *Variations on a Blue Guitar,* 206.

54. Greene, *Variations on a Blue Guitar,* 198.

55. Elwall, "Humanism in the Arts," 395f.

common life. Yet, to have a viable society, a humane common life is essential because the alternative is nearly unthinkable. Anarchy and chaos do not form a basis for society or civilization. The order she envisions is a democratic one where citizens hold their sense of freedom and responsibility in balance. Education in the arts plays a key role in that process. Her humanism is an applied humanism where relationships and institutions are guided by the desire to create a more peaceful and just society.

According to Greene, the artist is the voice of freedom throughout history. Because the artist makes known what was unknown, helps us to see what was unseen, and prods our imagination to consider what was not imagined, they have a vital role in the life of a community and nation. Furthermore, art is inexhaustible.[56] At the moment the public says, "Now I've seen it all," the artist creates something new. That happens because the artist discovers new ways of integrating the past with the present, old thoughts with new ones, and former modes of expression with a new dimension of feeling. We venerate the past if we incorporate the best of that tradition with new modes of expression. The two are linked in ways that make us aware of our own place in history and our roles in society. What is new is a remaking of what was present but unseen. In the same way, the artist takes material (clay, paint, light) and transforms it into an aesthetic experience. That experience holds the potential to transform us. Aesthetic moments speak directly to humane relationships and community. Art changes us; we change society, and that requires effort.

What we know of ancient civilizations is the art they created. We will be known in the same way by future generations. What we know of ourselves is found in the history that has brought us to this place, these ideas, this faith, this aesthetic. By experiencing artworks today, we know our civilization as others will know us in the future.

56. Greene, *Variations on a Blue Guitar*, 206.

3

Theatre and Applied Justice

In this chapter, I will explore several questions of applied aesthetic theory. Theatre historians across the globe focus considerable attention on the themes in drama, and this area of study is not polemical but empirical. Precisely, what is discovered by examining the themes in a play? A thematic investigation includes the sociopolitical context for a work of art—which means that this method of analysis is not strictly textual but also necessarily roams outside the text. Critical themes in drama explore the relationships between drama and sociopolitical trends.

> In a world that is unfinished, drama is used in lots of different ways—to increase understanding amongst audiences and participants, to highlight a common humanity, to encourage empathy and build resistance to oppressive regimes.[1]

These are keywords for this study: understanding, common humanity, empathy, and resistance. Empathy, as David Krasner points out, "allows us to transcend our world."[2] Theatre does all that! An in-depth study of theatre will discover such themes and

1. Freebody, *Critical Themes in Drama,* 206.
2. Krasner, "Empathy and Theatre," 256.

not avoid important considerations. To produce a play in our age requires the director, dramaturg, designers, and cast to carefully investigate the thematic aspects of a text. At the same time, it is worth remembering that examining themes in theatre does not sidestep other major elements such as character development, plot transitions, and language.

The examples that follow highlight a prominent theme: justice. And, if one considers the theories we have examined to this point, they all include justice as a major consideration. I am not referencing the justice system of judges, law enforcement, and such. My focus is on the just distribution of goods, political strategies, and the needs of a community. This is consistent with Aristotle's view of justice.[3] Plato had a different focus. Plato lauds the state. Aristotle is primarily concerned with the distribution of goods, integrity in the marketplace, the nature of goodness, and wisdom. He insists that justice means social equity and injustice is inequity.[4] Kant observes that aesthetic good is closely aligned with moral goodness. Heidegger points out that the arts disclose rift lines in society. Dickie is closely tied to the economic value of the arts by showing how art markets function. Danto examines the history of the West and its moment of exhaustion. Douglas Adams examines religious perspectives in the arts as a key to building community, and Maxine Greene is interested in pedagogy for a humane society.

Justice is fairness, said John Rawls,[5] and every child knows that is true. Go to any playground, and if one child creates even a minor playground infraction, you will hear, "That's not fair!" For adults who have even an inkling of social responsibility, fairness is not just a concept but an action. Fairness, in an unfair situation, is accompanied by restorative action. Fairness, for Rawls, implies that there are expectations for our personal behavior and standards for how social institutions relate to society's members. In Aristotle's view, justice does not just imply a fair distribution

---

3. Aristotle, *The Nicomachean Ethics*, 112ff.

4. Aristotle, *The Nicomachean Ethics*, 114.

5. Rawls, *A Theory of Justice*, 18.

of goods and fair treatment by the laws of the land. Justice also obligates a government or individual to rectify wrongs that have been committed.[6] That is a tough order. To argue that plays address the concerns of justice, including equity and restoration, is an even tougher claim. Yet I would argue that theatre has served both as a witness to and an agent for justice. Cornell West reminds us that "Justice is what love looks like in public."[7] Theatre provides a public face for both the unjust and the just acts of an era because one of its functions is to serve as a mirror to society.

The theatre should be entertaining, of course. But that does not mean this is the only way to experience it. Frankly, if you consider all the work that is required for a production, it had better be more than entertainment. Or, to put it another way, good entertainment can probably be found without the strenuous work of mounting a show. All the rehearsals, line memorizations, character studies, set and costume construction, stage management, lighting designs, makeup and wigs, program designers, proofreaders, publicity specialists, and box office activity must work in relative harmony to produce a show. That happens because the possibility for transformation occurs with a performance. Transformation is controversial because it opens the gates to the future, to the unknown, to vistas not yet seen.

I have covered only theatre in this section because that is my specialty. Of course, there are corollaries with other art forms, but in this section, theatre is the main area of investigation.

Theatre has traditionally had a fundamental role in serving as an agent for justice, illustrating how order is created from chaos. This is true for the first known scripted play, *The Persians*, by Aeschylus. It may come as a surprise that a retired Greek general would pen a work so sympathetic to the defeated Persians and critical of the Greek victors. Not only did Aeschylus write the play, but the city of Athens awarded it first prize for best play in 472 BCE. Many soldiers who fought in that war would have been in

6. Aristotle, *The Nicomachean Ethics*, 5. *The Code of Hammurabi* (1700 BCE) identifies restoration steps following an injustice.

7. Cornel West, quoted in Williams, "#In Context: Cornel West."

the audience. Imagine what might have happened if an American general in the Vietnam War had written a play eight years later praising the Communist People's Army of Vietnam. And what if that play had received the highest award in the land? My imagination is not large enough to think of that as a possibility. Reflect then on how deeply the Greeks must have believed in the freedom of speech. The function of the play in performance is to illustrate how war upsets the stability of the world and is the cause of unending destruction.

But Aeschylus is not alone. The long arm of theatre as justice stretches across the millennia, from the ancients to the contemporary world. In the nineteenth and twentieth centuries, writers such as Harriet Beecher Stowe, Wole Soyinka, Eugene O'Neill, Rhiannon Giddens, and Larissa FastHorse have contributed to justice and the arts tradition.

Harriet Beecher Stowe

It may seem odd, even implausible, to turn to Harriet Beecher Stowe's novel *Uncle Tom's Cabin* (1852) as an example of justice and theatre. William Wells Brown, a fugitive slave, gave a positive view of this work by stating that the play and the publicity "prepared the audience for things African."[8] I invite the reader to consider my analysis with this admonition: the play should no longer be staged anywhere. The "suffering Tom," who swayed the audiences prior to the Civil War, is nowadays seen as weak. Today, Tom is a symbol not of a free, proud, and dignified man, but of the opposite. The conformity of the novel and the play to nineteenth-century melodrama is another major weakness. That style has not translated well as history moved beyond the Civil War. Furthermore, even though Stowe was an abolitionist, her depiction of Blacks is now considered racist. But the history of this work is instructive, and one should venture forward with a recognition of the controversies that hover over Stowe and her novel. And because it is so

8. Brown, *William Wells Brown*, 284.

controversial, we might be able to learn more from it than from a humdrum work. It is a case study from the fossils of the stage.

In one sense, the early function of *Uncle Tom's Cabin* illustrates Hegel's thesis that the arts are the "spirit" that drives history. Secondly, it serves as an example of how a work of art can change in meaning over time and thereby fail to measure up to Kant's principle of durability. Whether it is useful to discuss *Uncle Tom's Cabin* to illustrate those two realities is open for discussion. The alternative might be to hide the play deep in the wings of a theatre where it never comes into the light. I believe that an honest assessment of the legacy of slavery can be instructive if we want to understand how race divides a society and vilifies marginalized persons.

Stowe's serialized novel was adapted for the stage even before her last chapter was published. By 1853, the adaptation by George L. Aiken had prevailed over all others. Today, of course, the play is never staged, and one hopes it will not be. But in its time, before the Civil War, it had a considerable impact on the public. It is that influence that I think is instructive. The play was immediately embraced by the abolitionists, and Stowe herself contributed to abolitionist causes. Her father, Lyman Beecher, is often credited for planting the seeds that blossomed into the abolitionist movement. There were thirteen children in the family, and nine became writers for the abolitionist cause. One of Harriet's brothers, Henry Ward Beecher, was such an ardent abolitionist that his church, Riverside Congregational Church in New York City, sent rifles to Black churches in Wamego, Kansas.[9] The boxes were labeled "Bibles," and nearly all made it to their intended destination. Another brother, Edward, moved to Michigan and Illinois to organize the abolitionist movement there at a time when many states were leaning toward support of the Fugitive Slave Act of 1850. The Beecher family did not fear their critics, who roundly attacked the family for supporting the abolitionist cause.

When the play opened on Broadway in 1853, the abolitionists posted tables in the lobby of the theatre to gather signatures

9. "Beecher Bible and Rifle Church."

to support their cause. They reported that nearly all the patrons signed the petition after exiting the theatre. That cannot be documented, but we do know that the numbers were vast. Those petitions were sent weekly to Congressional leaders in Washington, DC, and in the days before polling, signed petitions carried considerable weight. The play was so successful that it had nine performances each week from 1853 to the beginning of the Civil War in 1861 when it closed. To this day, it is still one of the longest-running plays in American history (some musicals have run longer). After the war, there were a few attempts to restage it, and a silent film (1902) was made with the George Aiken script, but it was not successful.

Uncle Tom's Cabin has a unique reputation in theatre and American history. No other sensational play has ever fallen from grace in such a spectacular way. It began as a celebrated work for abolitionists, and after the firing of the first shot at Fort Sumter, it became a theatrical pariah. Reactions to the play after the Civil War were often the opposite of what they had been prior. What had been a play against injustice was viewed later as an enabler of injustice. After 1861, it was hardly ever produced again. Sometimes, a thematic play passes into oblivion when the conditions that gave it life cease to exist. Today, it should be read as a relic of the antebellum era, which informs us of the horrors of slavery. *Uncle Tom's Cabin* has not passed the test of time as described by Immanuel Kant. The legacy of slavery survives to this day as a chronic illness in the American public body. Along this line, it is informative to read Michelle Alexander's *The New Jim Crow*, which chronicles the legacy of racism that followed the Civil War.

The question that still hangs over Stowe and all the abolitionists is their understanding of Black life and culture. They were opposed to slavery, but did they view minorities as equal to Whites or inferior? Did their commitment to the cause of freedom reflect an attitude of equality of the races? Once again, fugitive slave writer William Wells Brown (1814–84) is instructive when he records his personal experience of racism among abolitionists.[10]

10. Brown, *William Wells Brown*, 55.

I conclude this section on Stowe with the belief that the injustices of the past, as horrible as they were, need to be studied with the hope that we can avoid similar missteps. The lesson: a play that functioned as a moral battle cry in one era can become repugnant in the next. There are risks every time anyone begins to address these issues.

The stage adaptations of *Uncle Tom's Cabin* illustrate how plays that are highly thematic often change meaning when the conditions in society change.[11] That reality raises a question that the artist often faces. What are those conditions that will make a work of art resonate and sometimes define an era while others, maybe just as skillfully done, fail to connect in the same way? How is it that some playwrights seem to identify the rift lines of their age and have the skill to disclose the forces that reside below the surface in the tectonic plates in society? Why do some plays seem topically sequestered in their era while others have universal appeal across time and space? The answers to those questions probably cannot be answered in this short study. So, I will give you Kant's answer. Some artworks are universal because they support his claim that "Beautiful art is only possible as a product of *genius*."[12] There is no other word for it.

Wole Soyinka

After examining Stowe's abolitionist melodrama, we go to Africa and consider the impact of colonialism. Wole Soyinka's *Death and the King's Horseman* (1975)[13] explores what happens when local Yoruban rituals in Nigeria are interrupted by colonial leaders. The result is a nation that devolves into chaos until the king's son returns from London and enacts the traditional rites of death. Then, the community is restored to wholeness. Soyinka clearly spells out that the failure to follow the rituals of the culture creates more than

11. Another excellent example is Hermann Sudermann's play *Magda*.
12. Kant, *Critique of Judgment*, 150.
13. Soyinka, *Death and the King's Horseman*.

just a disorder in the human community. It is cosmic. Even the cosmos succumbs to chaos. Stability only returns after the death rituals are completed.

The play is a plea for cross-cultural compassion. By learning to know one another, humans form a new relationship that moves beyond tolerance toward understanding. When new bonds are formed across cultures, catharsis occurs. The infection disappears when the medicine works.

In Yoruban culture, when a king died, his horseman also needed to die, and the two men were buried together. Because the British colonial administrator, Pilkings, opposed this tradition, he ordered Elesin, the horseman, not to cause his own death. What ensues is a series of troubles that fall on Elesin and the tribe. Elesin is captured by slave traders and imprisoned where slaves were formerly held. Elesin's son, Olunde, is in England studying to become a physician, and when he hears the troubles back home, he returns to Nigeria. Once there, he faces humiliation and alienation because his father refused to follow the tradition. Eventually, both Elesin and Olunde commit suicide—which ends their family line and brings an end to the ritualistic sacrifice. In this way, Yoruban culture is slowly destroyed by the colonizers because they have disrupted the spiritual lives of the people. That was the aim of Pilkings, who saw all local customs as a violation of his own beliefs. As an emissary of colonialism, Pilkings has no self-awareness about the harm his beliefs have caused. In that sense, Soyinka discloses the injustices of colonialism and its destructive impact on the Yoruban people. The play is a plea to restore justice even when there is little hope that it will come. As Elesin observes, "Life is honor. It ends when honor ends."[14] That, Soyinka says, is the fate Africa refuses to accept.

Plays operate on two levels. The text shows what is audible and serves as a guide for the actors. But the meaningful dimension of a play can be subtext, the unspoken "force that drives the flower" and guides the characters subjectively. In Soyinka's play, the text explores where the colonists and the local population

14. Soyinka, *Death and the King's Horseman*, 15.

intersect. The subtext presents the power of colonialism, which drives the action and the local opposition to it. Colonialism and prejudice are subtextual themes in the story. While on the surface, the plot is about social traditions and disobedience of the Yoruban deities, beneath the surface, other forces are at work. The text emphasizes human failure to obey the gods (remember *Antigone*), but the subtext underscores the death of Yoruban culture under colonial rule. The play indicts the colonial rulers and the injustices of their administration. On the surface, at the textual level, colonialism appears to be benign and without sharp teeth. Beneath the surface, in the subtext, the violence of colonialism is a cause of trauma and the destruction of African traditions. The Yoruba are an ethnic group in Africa, but their life under colonialism symbolizes the condition of oppressed people around the world. Do similar patterns of dominance and expected submission also exist in America? Eugene O'Neill saw those troubled waters.

Eugene O'Neill (1888–1953) wrote plays that plumbed deep personal crises and troubling political realities in the United States. From his early staged work, such as *Moon of the Caribbees* (written in 1917, produced 1918) to his final play, *A Moon for the Misbegotten* (written in 1943, produced 1957), O'Neill addresses conditions of injustice. Yet his plots do not end with the characters mired in that situation; he often provides a window into the future, a future where the suffering of the victims will end. In 1924, his play about interracial marriage, *All God's Chillun Got Wings*, opened in New York.[15] Miscegenation was against the law in many states, and to cause an additional stir, the Black husband embraced and kissed the hands of his White wife. Numerous critics thought the play stirred up controversy when that might have been avoided. It was banned in the South. Many American cities had experienced racial conflagrations following World War I, and O'Neill's play brought racial issues into the theatre. He exposed the pain and suffering inflicted by Jim Crow laws, and despite the critics, O'Neill stood firm in his conviction that the nation needed his play.

15. O'Neill, *The Plays of Eugene O'Neill*, vol. 2.

All God's Chillun Got Wings is a realistic play with a tone of pathos that envelops the main characters. Jim and Ella, a young married couple, struggle in their marriage due to the disease of prejudice. Their interracial marriage becomes a metaphor for the nation. The political temper of the times was chaos, and this was not the first time O'Neill had put his oar into that raging sea. The lead character, a Black man named Jim Harris, is preparing to pass the bar exam, which his wife thinks may not happen in Jim Crow America. But Jim believes in the foundational principles of his country and pursues his dream. More importantly, he relishes the social status it will provide for him. But his preparation is haphazard. In his single-minded obsession with this dream, the racial gap in society creeps into their marriage. Deep down, he knows he will never be accepted in White society.

The character Jim was played by the actor Paul Robeson, who had passed the bar exam! Emotions ran high, and the tensions in the marriage became unbearable until Ella screamed at the world, "Why don't you let Jim and me be happy?" That "you" has reference to the racial heritage of Jim Crow America. Jim fails the exam, and instead of feeling crushed, he and Ella celebrate. Jim accepts himself as he is and is no longer obsessed with his goal. The problem was not his aspiration but his fixation that caused him to ignore those around him. The anxiety is gone from their lives, and so they return to the love that initially brought them together. Jim is no longer preoccupied with his goal while ignoring all others, and Ella no longer loses him to his fixation. Jim's pursuit of the legal profession was not the issue. Rather, the problem was his obsession with it while ignoring the person who loved him the most.

O'Neill is warning that the racial hatred that resides in the hearts of many American citizens will lead to hostilities that change our national ethos. The narrative asks the audience to reconsider how social pressures surrounding race can cause despair and how individuals, as well as the nation overall, can possibly move beyond the morass of racial prejudice. Only when Jim and Ella face their situation and stop pretending that race does not matter can they experience the catharsis that love engenders. Again and yet, there is also pathos because the play depicts a talented Black man in the 1920s still shackled by Jim Crow and struggling to find the America that keeps promising equality and justice.

O'Neill's use of dialect in this play and others has been criticized. I join that crowd in recognizing that his written dialect may come across as insensitive or just simply off the mark. Even his Irish-dialect plays were critiqued by the Irish for his version of the accent. He presents another case where we can both recognize his contribution and accept his flaws.

Two years earlier, in 1922, his play *Emperor Jones* opened in New York. That play was the first one on American soil where Black and White actors simultaneously shared the same stage. Prior to that, all Black characters in plays in the United States were played by Whites using blackface makeup. Paul Robeson also played the lead on stage in *Emperor Jones* and in the movie based on that production. O'Neill's courage in the face of American prejudice is not often considered when his plays are evaluated. His ability to put his finger on the pulse of the time contributed to some initial steps toward racial understanding.[16]

O'Neill carved out a special landscape for himself in the American theatre world. He challenged social injustices such as racism, economic disparities, and marginalization of minorities such as his own Irish heritage. To the surprise of critics and the disapproval of his father, the famous actor James O'Neill, he wrote his first plays in accented Irish brogue. Up to that point, his father had attempted to shed his Irishness, which meant leaving no trace of his former accent. The critics predicted that the accents would doom his plays, but O'Neill held firm. His agenda was larger than accents, heritage, and even racial disparity. He was, as Daniel Cawthon observes, writing to demonstrate that "Salvation comes from the artist, the poet, the playwright. O'Neill and his fellow artists are there to mediate, to unveil the inner secret of existence."[17] His agenda to unveil the truth parallels Heidegger's dictum that "art is truth revealing itself." Art asks of us, plain ordinary folk,

16. "Eugene O'Neill: A Controversial Play," *American Experience*, PBS.

17. Cawthon, "Eugene O'Neill," 29.

to consider the magnitude of ultimate reality: focus our attention, work, and being on the essence of existence. If we can do that, we participate, symbolically, in the ground of being, according to Paul Tillich.[18]

William Shakespeare

A vastly different approach to interracial marriage emerges in Shakespeare's *Othello*.[19] The significance of this work has shifted since the Elizabethan era. Then, the presence of a Moor was exotic and unusual; today, the play exposes the racial division in America where one side, the African, rises to greatness, only to be destroyed by the devious and vicious mechanisms so often inherent in White supremacy. In the same way that *Othello* follows an old tragic play-book—the flawed hero—the antagonist has been scripted with another: the reduction and possible elimination of someone who has risen above their social station. With the passing of time and the movement of people, the issues have changed from Shakespeare's time, but the script has not. Yet through those changes, the script survives as a vital text that illuminates the struggles of the current racial divide. So, how does *Othello* address justice as a desirable and obtainable goal?

The themes in *Othello* are well-known—betrayal, racism, gender, jealousy, murder, pathos. The play concludes with Othello recognizing his own tragic errors, which lead to the tragic ending. Iago devotes his energies to betraying Othello and advancing the notion that Desdemona is unfaithful. He warns Othello that Desdemona does not fully comprehend the true nature and intentions of a Moor. To that, Othello defends Desdemona and himself: "For she had eyes and chose me" (*Othello*, 3.3.203). Othello, who trusts Iago on the battlefield, also trusts him in this moment of treachery. It's a fatal mistake because he falls more deeply into Iago's abyss of deception. The love between Othello and Desdemona is shredded

---

18. Tillich, *On Art and Architecture*, 37.

19. My remarks here on Shakespeare are slightly revised from my essay in Friesen and Koehn, eds., *Anabaptist ReMix*, 137–65.

by lies from Iago and a growing suspicion on the part of Othello until matters reach a shattering point: Othello acts by killing his wife. Only then does he learn that his great weakness, naiveté, has destroyed his life, fortune, and hope. Othello reveals his agony:

> He that filches from me my good name
> Robs me of that which not enriches him,
> And makes me poor indeed. (3.3.172–74)

After the murder, Othello takes responsibility for his own gullibility and actions, but it does not bring about a sense of equilibrium because he has destroyed Desdemona and thereby doomed himself. To regain his honor by killing his wife, he has lost his honor.

For modern audiences, the destructive force of racism practically overwhelms any consideration of justice and injustice in Shakespeare's *Othello*. Early in the play's action, Brabantio hints at this in a prelude to Iago's trickery and use of innuendo. In the face of all the accusations Iago levels against his wife, Othello remains noble in intention and just in his actions until the final deed when he kills Desdemona. His action underscores Iago's diabolical stance that a Moor, even a highly capable military leader, is too gullible and emotional to understand the human heart. "Othello's sense of honor is intimately bound up with his belief in justice."[20] But this does not prevent a just and gallant hero from falling victim to gossip and the vile tactics of lesser men. That fall is the tragedy of Othello, and Shakespeare has the skill to develop the plot whereby fear and pity are presented with magnitude. Overcome with jealousy, Othello kills Desdemona. When he learns, too late, that his wife is blameless, he asks to be remembered as one who "loved not wisely but too well" (5.2.354) and kills himself. We are presented with an ending that illustrates the great waste of human goodness. We weep for both Desdemona and Othello, both of whom fall victim to Iago's depraved devices. Shakespeare presents a heroic African who is honored by many, except one, Iago, who is intent on bringing him down. He uses treachery and

20. Orkin, "Othello and the 'Plain Face' of Racism," 172.

the Moor's weakness of jealousy to destroy two lives. Shakespeare never has to say it explicitly, but he understands the tactics and motivation of White supremacy. In fact, Iago's character and words align themselves with the villainy of White supremacy. The parallel methods in America have been lynching and police brutality, but the objective is the same: destroy the Black man and his family to set an example for all others. Early in the play, these words by Iago to Brabantio, father of Desdemona, may as well be the prologue to the ancient American racist taboo against interracial marriage:

> Even now, now, very now, an old black ram
> Is tupping your white ewe. Arise, arise;
> Awake the snorting citizens with the bell,
> Or else the devil will make a grandsire of you. (1.1.90–93)

Shakespeare unmasks those tactics for all to see. We, the audience, become witnesses and are thereby challenged to act against those tactics for justice to prevail. Shakespeare exposes White supremacy as a condition that destroys trust, human relationships, and institutions. As Brigitte Fielder[21] notes, with the marriage of a Black man and a White woman, Shakespeare exposes the racist horrors of his audience.

Othello slices the principle of justice in different ways than the plays we have examined so far. It illustrates the tyranny of the lie, a lie repeated and augmented by even greater lies until a valiant and just hero is erased. Iago has used his tongue to destroy the life and liberty of others, and he is devoid of any effort to rectify the situation. In the wake of Othello's fall, political instability and chaos will possibly ensue. It is a warning from William Shakespeare that political leadership, especially by an honorable leader, can be wiped out by intrigue, suspicion, and diabolical defamations, especially when these are tossed into a cauldron of racial tension. A kingdom without justice is a realm corroding from within.

Justice and Aristotle's catharsis both occur when the audience recognizes their own culpability in a world of treachery and reflects on their own errors in judgment and action. Othello appeals

---

21. Fielder, "Blackface Desdemona," 47.

in vain to a transcendent being who might rescue him. But the play shows that justice is a human responsibility. We need to differentiate expressions of love, such as Desdemona's, from Iago's betrayal under the guise of loyalty and friendship. Iago's character is cleverly identified by Andy Mousley: "A human being devoid of emotion is no human being."[22] Iago's inhumanity and diabolical scheming lie at the core of the plot. Shakespeare removes responsibility for justice from the heavenly realm and brings it down to earth. Humans need to learn and then act justly. Othello is caught between the ethic of duty and the freedom of discernment. Duty to the city brought him honor; duty to his fears led to destruction. He believed when he should have doubted. Shakespeare warns us against falling into that trap. Shakespeare sounds the alarm on the tragic power of racism, which he saw lurking, ready to pounce, in the shadows of civilization. Racism thrives on fear of the other and self-pity. This, I remind you, illustrates Aristotle's fear and guilt paradigm for tragedy.

Larissa Fasthorse

Sometimes, a change of pace is needed to lift the soul from sorrow. A new playwright, Larissa FastHorse, has the skill to do that. She explores the tensions and resolutions of rituals surrounding the Thanksgiving celebration in the United States.[23] In *The Thanksgiving Play* (2015), she challenges the audience with historical details that are frequently omitted when this holiday is celebrated, and she also addresses the role Native Americans played as the European settlers began to claim territory in the Americas. With humor, she exposes the falsehoods that have made this holiday so significant for many and so painful for others, especially the dislocation of people who lived and prospered on this continent for millennia. The humor in the play avoids mocking the settlers as it discloses their shortcomings and less than altruistic motives. But do not be

22. Mousley, *Re-Humanizing Shakespeare*, 59.
23. FastHorse, *The Thanksgiving Play*.

mistaken; this is not a lighthearted comedy—the humor bites, and it bites deep. The cast is all White, and their job is to prepare children for a Native heritage program at school. The audience slowly begins to realize that this is a joke because the grownups do not know how to prepare the children for the program. FastHorse ridicules shallow attempts at inclusion and diversity when there is no visible inclusion or diversity. Her play also illustrates the wide cultural divide between the settlers and the first peoples in this land. Silence, for example, often makes Europeans uncomfortable, who prefer to fill empty conversational spaces with voices. By contrast, the character Jaxton highlights the power of silence: "By silencing Native voices, we have made them too strong. Silence is so powerful on stage. Our characters cannot compete with that."[24] Thus, the play appeals to understanding across the cultural spectrum and centuries of conflict. Perhaps the long divide can be closed, and broken relationships can be restored.

The unrealized hope in this work provides a window for a future where justice will prevail. Justice as wholeness requires effort and demands new understanding. In many cases, it will challenge our own self-identity. In her review of this show, Helen Shaw notes the "largely white audience, white-led producing theatre, and the white collaborators are all part of the punch line."[25] The celebration of heritage, while essentially excluding people of that heritage in the celebration, is the focus of the playwright's critique.

The settlers possibly never comprehended the basic elements of Native culture. The harm they cause is rooted in a total lack of interest in learning about local cultural traditions. Their obtuseness empowers Native voices to reclaim their heritage and the narrative of Thanksgiving. It was not simply a day for them because giving thanks was a way of life. A comic rendition of a tragic episode can bite into our psyche and become memorable in disturbing ways. It is disruptive because it points to the injustices of the past and our inability to redress them. We experience guilt because of our nation's past and feel fear because the path to

24. FastHorse, *The Thanksgiving Play*, 57.
25. Shaw, "On Broadway," 7.

justice is complicated. Catharsis may not be attainable unless we can laugh at our own shortcomings. When rift lines are exposed so deftly, laughter signals catharsis. We cannot change history. Even ignoring it does not erase it, and laughter does not excuse anyone from responsibility for the current situation. Opera and musicals can have a similar impact. History is what it is, and now that we know it, what will we do about it?

Lin-Manuel Miranda

Like FastHorse, Lin-Manuel Miranda (1980–) has also applied his playwriting gift to the problems of American history, and his Broadway musical about Alexander Hamilton likewise appeared in 2015. *Hamilton* uses a mix of hip-hop and other musical genres in a play costumed and set in the Revolutionary era. It references Hamilton's marginal Caribbean identity and rise to attain considerable influence on George Washington as well as major federal and financial institutions in the early American Republic. The theatre critic David Cote summed up his entire experience this way: "I love *Hamilton*. I love it like I love New York or Broadway when it gets it right. And this is so right. A sublime conjunction of radio-ready hip hop (as well as R&B, Britpop, and trade showstoppers), under-dramatized American history, and Miranda's uniquely personal focus as a first-generation Puerto Rican and inexhaustible wordsmith, *Hamilton* hits multilevel culture buttons, hard. . . . The work's human drama and novelistic density remain astonishing."[26] Cote's gushing response was nearly universal because the production was so strong on emotional transmission from stage to the audience—even though more than one critic noted the weak plot, which explores the conflict between Aaron Burr and Alexander Hamilton with many subplots along the way. The tension, and eventual duel, between Burr and Hamilton, ends fatefully and brings the evening to a close in this award-winning production.

---

26. Cote, "Theatre Review: 'Hamilton,'" 21.

With *Hamilton*, Lin-Manuel Miranda demonstrated that transfiguration could occur even in our own history. While the Founding "Fathers" are usually relegated to heroic and mythic status, Miranda illustrates their humanity, including flaws. The one character who rises above the swirl of egos and greed is Hamilton's wife, Eliza. She is the stable throughline in the script and repeatedly calms the waters. In reference to Eliza, Miranda says that she brought contemporary compassion to the historical narrative. In other words, she is the key to the plot. According to Miranda, the issues we face today are similar to those Hamilton faced: the role of women in a democracy, the reality of immigration, the legacy of slavery and its far-reaching evils, and the proper function of the federal government and a central banking system. He says, "This is a story about America then, told by America now, and we want to eliminate any distance between a contemporary audience and this story."[27] It was and remains a story that is highly expressive while distancing itself from prior styles and forms of musical theatre.

The end of art means the conclusion of a tradition, which also means the beginning of a new one. A reader reaches the final page of a novel and looks for the sequel. That sequel may cast a light on what else might be visible. Danto suggests that it will be a vibrant time, invigorated by pluralism and leaving behind former, more parochial, conventions.[28] This new page will no longer be constrained by tradition and may, in fact, only reach back to what is useful for a contemporary aesthetic. Old norms and expectations as to what art is and how it should be will no longer maintain their grip. As a result, we are living in one of the most contentious and stirring times in all of art history. We are witnessing a renewed desire for catharsis, not as a free-floating feeling or attitude but rather as a sensibility linked with social and economic justice.[29] That is something to celebrate.

27. Miranda, quoted in Delman, "How Lin-Manuel Miranda Shapes History."

28. Danto, *After the End of Art*, 17.

29. Freebody and Finneran, *Critical Themes in Drama*.

The theatre was and continues to be a dedicated community. On the one hand, it is secular, and on the other, it is as sacred as any gathering. And in a theatre performance, those two hands clap. They clap with purpose as a resounding reality that art can plumb the depths of religion while guiding the community along the fault lines where human encounters exist. While human encounters are nearly always nonviolent, the potential for chaos and disruption is often present. Fault lines are often safe for walking: hold hands as you go, and maybe even spread a blanket for a picnic. But on those occasions when there is an eruption, everyone ducks, hides, or gets caught in the conflagration.

Rhiannon Giddens

For many music lovers, the Romantic era of opera, dominant for most of the nineteenth century, is held in high esteem. But the following example may burst that image. A new opera, *Omar*, had its premiere in 2022.[30] Cowritten and composed by Rhiannon Giddens (1977–) and Michael Abels (1962–), the story features an adult slave, Omar, who ran away a few months after arriving in the United States. After he was captured and imprisoned, he surprised the jailers and slave masters by writing selections of the Qur'an in Arabic on the prison cell wall. Apparently, many Whites in South Carolina had never encountered an African who could read and write. Omar had memorized lengthy passages of the Qur'an, which also made him seem exotic.

While still in jail, he was sold to a new owner, who appointed him to a more privileged status, but never freed him. Before his death at the age of ninety-three, he wrote his life story in Arabic. That story, originally written in 1831, is the basis for the opera. Bringing his story to life on stage is an act of justice for someone who never saw justice in this land. This new work restores his stature in the human family and provides another level of evidence that Africans have a strong sense of culture, religion, heritage, and

30. Hall, "Tell Your Story, Omar," 39–41.

identity. The scholar Hussein Rashid understands the impact of the opera:

> The way I understand this, and the way several other scholars understand this, . . . is that this is Omar talking about being enslaved, recognizing that it is other human beings playing at power, playing at having sovereignty, playing at having authority over other human beings. And he is saying, "No, you don't actually know what power is, you don't know what sovereignty is, you don't know where my allegiance is."[31]

Omar sees when others are blind. His resilience in the face of the great evils of slavery evokes feelings that are often suppressed in ways similar to the suppression of this historical narrative. It is an act of justice to recall our nation's past errors with the hope that we will gain freedom from the power of those shackles. Freedom only exists when people take responsibility for the issues that haunt the nation. In those moments, we recognize our common humanity and need to rectify a legacy of injustice. We have come a great distance only to discover Aristotle is also there.

These brief summaries of several playscripts serve as examples of aesthetic theories. They illustrate the complexity of judging artworks because local traditions, the passing of time, and changing social structures are all relevant for such an assessment. Maybe it is evident that each play has value and, within its context, has a legitimate place. All work can be seen as creative acts worthy of our attention. And in the passing of time, some will appear more worthy than others. They endure because they continue to evoke a response from those who encounter them.

This chapter began with a look at justice and how theatre witnesses to and is an agent for justice. The question that remains is whether the arts free us from the bondage of guilt and fear so that we can restore the truth of our own history. Catharsis happens in those moments.

---

31. Hussein Rashid, quoted in Tsioulcas, "The Debut of 'Omar,' a Thoroughly American Opera."

4

The Dialogue Continues

With Danto's declaration of the end of art, aesthetic analysis begins again. New beginnings should take into consideration a wider cultural perspective while at the same time acknowledging a debt to previous investigations, with the awareness that all people are one race—the human race, variations within the global community should be celebrated, not vilified. Former barriers often established by religious, linguistic, and national traditions have severe limits and stifle a quest for common bonds. Can a new aesthetic augment unique traditions and, at the same time, embrace the greater human community? It must, Danto replies.

Artists—and this is a generalization—are not interested in forming a community separate from culture, as some religious traditions have advocated. Christ is not in, above, against, or even through culture, as H. Richard Niebuhr proposed in his seminal study.[1] The arts, as a segment of culture, are in continual tension with religion, and in that state, a synthesis emerges that transcends both. For the synthesis to have integrity and endure, both the arts and religion need to remain authentic. Adding a piece of one to a piece of the other does not make a synthesis. Religion and the arts

---

1. Niebuhr, *Christ and Culture.*

84

thrive when they are actively engaged in dialogue with each other, not about, against, or above each other.

Another dimension, justice, respects both the artist's freedom and the freedom of religious expression. Cultural engagement is not a beautified phrase for oppressive domination but the opposite. Cultural engagement by artists is a methodology to initiate a dialogue between the community and the artist's work. No unitary system of justice can become operative for all people, all contexts, and all cultures. All cultures and religions have validity, heritage, and identity. A new aesthetic that can aid our global awareness is needed.

With all these perspectives in mind and the recognition that every author, especially this one, has limitations, I suggest the following: a renewed understanding of catharsis as a valid experience of meaningful artwork. Meaningful art is rooted in how well it gives voice to those who have been marginalized, oppressed, or victimized by social structures, legal systems, or religious authorities. Art, authentic art, generally arises as a response to those realities or describes those conditions. The new catharsis is experienced where justice prevails, and injustice is marginalized or eliminated. Fear and guilt are washed away when the cloud of injustice is lifted and hope restored. The arts function as an agent for justice simply by being significant art. What makes art significant? It reveals the rift lines in society and personal experience. No hidden or symbolic messages are needed because a didactic slant stifles catharsis rather than providing the experience of wholeness.

That journey from chaos to wholeness, from violence to peace, from oppression to liberation, is the agenda that the arts have addressed since their origin. With that recurring theme, there is also a new interest in redefining catharsis. The focus is not just on the individual patron and how they feel at the end of a production but on the wider impact on society. Recent theatrical work addresses social ills and not just personal foibles. Therefore, theatre has a role to play in creating wholeness for the greater community. This link with society is not just a contemporary concern because it has occurred frequently in history, as we have noted.

Justice is the handmaiden for catharsis. Unfair policies, practices, or judgments do not result magically in wholeness. No biblical miracle happened that way, either. In a speech given in 1853, less than a decade before the outbreak of the Civil War, Theodore Parker spoke to the Abolitionist Society of New York and delivered this memorable line, "I do not pretend to understand the moral universe; the arc is a long one, my eye reaches but little ways; I cannot calculate the curve and complete the figure by the experience of sight; I can divine it by conscience. And from what I see, I am sure it bends towards justice."[2] The arts are a witness to and an agent for that bending of history.

And, of course, justice is not all the arts do. The arts expose us to new feelings or make us aware of them for the first time. An actor once told Lloyd Richards, dean of the Yale Drama School, I cannot play Macbeth because I have never been angry enough to kill someone. Richards, according to his report, paused, then quietly asked him if he ever had a mosquito buzz in his ear. Another pause. Then Richards asked if it disturbed him enough to kill it. "Of course," the actor answered. "Then pretend Duncan is that mosquito," replied Dr. Richards. The actor, like many people, suppressed a lot of anger but failed to recognize it, acknowledge it, and know its destructive power.

Becoming aware of negative emotions is the first step toward wholeness. The arts can make us aware of our inner selves so that we might avoid acting out our own destructive impulses. The stage is the greatest educational institution that teaches us the folly of human destruction! The alternative, nonviolent action, is a mark of wholeness, and wholeness is catharsis.

Expressiveness

The end of the Western tradition, as viewed by Danto, also marks the end of expressive forms. The rigid constructions of Fredrick Schiller, Richard Brinsley Sheridan, Jean Racine, or Joost van den

2. "Theodore Parker," Wikipedia.com.

Vondel no longer resonate with the spirit of our time. They have become museum works. At the same time, the sprawling and undisciplined expressiveness of the Romantics is also dated and no longer grasps our attention. The prevailing view is that Victor Hugo's nine-hour *Hernani* (1830) cannot be staged. The Romantic movement spawned plays where human instinct and excessive emotionalism were dripping over the stage apron. Many have assumed they went too far in their rejection of controlled classicism. Eventually, though, their sprawling texts were clipped, set to music, and found their natural venues in opera and contemporary melodrama. Those works follow conventional theatrical forms that hark back to the Greek tragedies, comedies, and satyr plays. They now have their own niche on the cultural scene but are no longer viewed as innovative theatre.

Now, at the end of art, the forefront in theatre is highly thematic while subverting form and sometimes even expressiveness. Topics dominate. Tony Kushner and Paula Vogel place LGBTQ issues center stage with, respectively, *Angels in America* (1991–92) and *How I Learned to Drive* (1997). George C. Wolfe asks audiences to come to terms with racial prejudice with his in-your-face *Colored Museum* (1986) and *Bring in 'da Noise/Bring in 'da Funk* (1995). The opera tradition has been adapted in several nontraditional works, such as Jonathan Larson's *Rent* (1996) and Baz Luhrmann's *La Bohème* (1993), which are both loose adaptations of Puccini's work. Their new emphasis zeroes in on the oppressive nature of poverty. The search for expressiveness continues by moving beyond the formalist structures from classical, neoclassical, or modernist traditions and into hip-hop and rock. Thematic expression, for its own sake, has become the postmodern life of the stage. The *end* of art, therefore, is not the same as the *death* of art. Instead, it recognizes a shift in how art is created, viewed, and critiqued.[3] The recognition and validation of that shift are crucial for Danto.

Current theatrical works rely less on symbolism (Ibsen), allegory (W. B. Yeats), and religious orthodoxy (T. S. Eliot) and

3. Danto, *After the End of Art*, 4.

directly address the sorrow, rage, and hope inherent in social and political conditions. August Wilson's memorable line, "I want my ham!" from *Two Trains Running* (1990), rings in the ears of all who have witnessed a powerful interpretation of his character, Hambone. This repeated line becomes the call and response for justice in a manner much like a Black gospel service. Wilson and many postmodern playwrights employ devices from a variety of cultural references as they seek to develop the expressiveness of their characters. In a comparable way, Luis Valdez relies on Chicano culture and its references to enrich his narratives. His *El Fin del Mundo* (1973) begins when the character Mundo Mata overdoses and enters the land of the dead. There, he encounters prior friends and acquaintances who try to convince him to become the lord of the dead. When the effect of the drugs wears off, Mata renews his commitment to the world of the living. While the setting is mythological, the play is about the clash between myth and reality.

Wilson and Valdez expose the frailty of the human soul as they portray the vulnerability of marginal people. Their characters have lost hope—which is why they resort to unusual tactics when addressing their situations. Hambone wants to confront the man who cheated him but cannot muster the courage to do so. Mata wants to escape from the despairing conditions that surround him. In the end, both major characters present a challenge to the audience: what direction would you take if you faced similar circumstances? Will we, the viewers, find a way past our own situations to act? Both authors are waiting, metaphorically, to hear from you.

Suzan-Lori Parks's recent *Plays for the Plague Year* (2023)[4] employs seldom-used theatrical devices, which makes it difficult to describe—difficult because each performance depends on audience participation. At the beginning of the evening, the stage manager distributes paper and pens to each audience member and gives a single prompt: write a sentence about your memory of the year of COVID-19. It is very open-ended, and after the brief writing exercise, the papers are collected, and they form the narrative of the play, which proceeds as a memory play and contextual

4. Parks, *Plays for the Plague Year*.

conversation. All the comments begin with observations from the audience that night. The play unfolds until Parks concludes it with her own creative narrative. Audience members participate in this group ritual, which contemporizes the immediate past. All memories are valid, and thus, each person understands anew their place in society and possibly discovers a sense of purpose. Throughout the dialogue, Parks weaves in detail from her own life and reading. As a result, critic Maya Phillips notes, "'Theater does not save us,' the writer says, 'but it does preserve us somehow,' so this piece is a record. This is catharsis. It is preservation."[5] Preservation as catharsis is a reassuring possibility when truncated from its classical scaffolding.

Community

I have veered far from my claim that theatre is a committed community. So a few explanations are needed.

The reason theatre communities are so committed is because they have common ownership in the production. Yes, ownership. The production is larger than any individual, and yet each one is vital to its life and being. The cast, crew, management, and janitors are all dedicated to a common product. At one level, they do not ask about differences in politics, religion, ethnicity, or first language. Those issues are pushed into the background so that the art can be brought to life on the stage. The play, they believe, has its own being, and they are all responsible for breathing life into its lungs. Even though they do not place weight on their differences, they allow for room to discuss them during relaxing times. Success at the box office and positive reviews will often increase dedication to the production the company creates. Increased salaries, scholarships, or other benefits aid company morale. Thus, strong bonds can also form through informal friendships, but that is not necessary for a vital production. Shared values can also contribute

5. Phillips, "Review: In 'Plays for the Plague Year,' the Soundtrack of Our Lives."

to company harmony. Common ownership, though, is only one factor in the long theatrical tradition in Western cultures.

Institutional values, though, do not tell the full story. There are many reasons why theatre companies are highly dedicated to their work. We can easily put aside common perceptions that it is an ego trip for performers and nothing more. Yes, that might happen, and probably every stage has fed that indulgence, but that is not enough to sustain a heritage for nearly two and a half millennia. What sustains the tradition is the creation of a world the audience and company can dwell in, even if for an evening or a long run. For that reason, and almost for that reason alone, theatre artists commit their time and sometimes money to live in the world where those characters live. There are necessary ingredients: a narrative, language, spectacle, and audience connections to create the world of play. All those elements fall into place when imagination, feelings, and thought coalesce. It is the possibility of transfiguring the commonplace into another world that has its own being.

Plays in production establish their own space and time. Sometimes, years are condensed into a few hours, and rarely, if ever, does the time within a play correspond to the actual playing time. Audiences, and even the performers, suspend our natural inclinations regarding time and space. We accept the painted foam rocks as real boulders, the cardboard crowns as real ones, and our imaginations are not limited by the actual walls of a theatre. The same is true for time. Arthur Miller's *Playing for Time* (1980) employs that device with sensitive skill. The play is set in a World War II death camp that has an orchestra. The Jewish players are confined to the camp and expected to play at the beck and call of German camp managers. Slowly, one musician after another disappears: they exit, die offstage, and are not replaced. Eventually, the play ends when the musicians are too weak to play. All this takes place in little more than an hour of performance time because Miller deftly condensed the time of the historical episode. Why is that play done? Entering that world and learning of that fault line creates an awareness we wish and yet do not wish to know. We try to stand on two sides of that fault line, and eventually, the quake forces the audience to one side (oppressors) or the other (victims). There is no escape, no exit.

After the audience exits the theatre, they cannot escape what they encountered. A powerful theatre piece will hang over audience members like a heavy cloud, even though the sun is shining. Those who reflect on the experience will soon recognize that in some, even possibly nondiscursive manner, they were transformed by the experience. An hour before the curtain was raised, they were thinking about lunch or dinner. But now, after an encounter with one of the rift lines in history, they have become aware of the tectonic plates that shift, clash, and reshape the world. Even though a tragic play evokes strong emotions in audiences, lighter works often have the same impact. People will often not recall what they ate a week ago but remember in detail the first time they saw *Oklahoma!* (1943). Is *Oklahoma!* a tectonic-shifting work? Maybe not, maybe so. A show that is so memorable will keep shifting in the memory boxes and have an impact long after it was experienced. Yes, *Oklahoma!* I contend that it centers on one of America's tectonic plates: recent settlers trying to maintain community as they struggle against tradition, the weather, marginal incomes, and disruptive behaviors.

When our inner life is shaped so strongly by the arts, we need to acknowledge that the transformation that occurs makes us more aware of our common humanity. This is the foundation for the community. It is the creation of such a community that motivates many theatre artists to put up with unending, exhausting, challenging rehearsals to create such a work. When the final curtain comes down after the last show, the impact of that show is hardly over for the community that encountered its world.

The arts are like the tallgrass prairie, which pierces the topsoil with twelve-foot roots and bonds together to form a stable environment for many forms of life. The theatre also pierces deeply through the surfaces of human experience to create a common bond whereby people can recognize a common humanity. That recognition is catharsis, wholeness, and beauty. Frequently, "theatre penetrates and uncovers wounds, causing tears."[6] Tears can enable us to see humanity in a new light. And that awareness, as we have seen, is often a sign of transformation. To be fully human is a reference to the aesthetic dimension of life because people are a cultural and biological species.[7]

One of the more interesting developments in this "end of art" era is the focus on themes in theatre. In the past, theatre publications tended to focus on structure, style, and type. Today, the trend is leaning, maybe even lurching, toward social themes. Recent plays have taken the lead, but scholarship has quickly followed their example. Plays, starting with Bertolt Brecht, focused on economic justice in *The Good Woman of Setzuan* (1943) and the wastefulness of war in *Mother Courage and Her Children* (1941). Marsha Norman in *"Night Mother"* (1983) examines the prevalence of suicide among young women. Numerous playwrights have drawn attention to LGBTQ issues, including William M. Hoffman with *As Is* (1985), Larry Kramer with *The Normal Heart* (1985), and Paul Vogel with *Indecent* (2015). Their plays have had many revivals. Racial awareness and Black history have also taken center stage in many theatres. August Wilson's *The Pittsburgh Cycle* (1982–2005), comprised of ten separate plays, has been among the most notable and widely produced. The young playwright Lynn Nottage has won numerous awards with *Intimate Apparel* (2003), which explores race and economic disparity. At what point does awareness of disparity become a justice issue? Religion has also been a major theme in several works, including the award-winning *The Book of Mormon* (2011) and John Patrick Shanley's *Doubt: A Parable* (2004). Musicals also placed religion front and center: Stephen Schwartz's *Godspell* and Andrew Lloyd-Webber's *Jesus Christ Superstar*, both initially produced in 1971.

Between 1979 and 1986, Cambridge University Press published an eight-volume study by James Redmond titled *Themes in Drama*. The series focused on religion, society, and philosophy. After his retirement, the press issued another eleven volumes in

6. Rood, *Theatre and Theology*, 355.
7. McClendon, Jr., *Ethics*, 93.

that series. This thematic approach will likely continue as a road-map for many playwrights and scholars in the future.

I make this prediction based on thirty-two years of teaching theatre history and aesthetics. As I shifted from teaching structure and style to investigating major themes in dramatic works, a new world opened for my students and me. Furthermore, in exploring themes in plays, students soon discovered how plays are structured, the strengths and limits of characters, and the major plot shifts. In other words, those Aristotelian elements that have formed the basis for teaching theatre can probably be discovered and taught most effectively by pursuing a thematic approach. Why is this method effective? So many themes resonate with issues students face: injustice, betrayal, greed, violence, lack of veracity, identity, family crises, and loss of hope. The thematic approach enables readers to discover how theatre, even ancient work, holds a mirror to our own time. With that discovery, students eagerly pursue the adjacent questions of structure and style.

Hope

The arts, and especially theatre, will continue to explore questions of justice. It seems evident that we need theatre to remind us repeatedly that our task is not just to maintain social systems (family, school, religion, neighborhood) but also to bring justice to those who have been wronged. That is how theatre functions at its best and can contribute to the larger society.

There have always been efforts by governments and religious leaders to place limits on what is acceptable and approved art. Those efforts are seldom effective. The early church prohibited theatre, and what happened was the rise of the traveling minstrel, folk poetry, and even clown shows. The greatest historical irony is that the very church that banned theatre gave rise to it again in 923 CE when four monks in St. Gall, Switzerland, reenacted the narrative of the three women named Mary visiting the tomb and meeting the angel. As I have noted, the Puritans also attempted to abolish theatre only to have writers such as William D'Avenant circumvent those bans by staging plays set to music (operas). The Soviet Union placed writers under constant surveillance and oppression, but writers persisted by smuggling their works to publishers outside the country. That is how *The Gulag Archipelago* by Aleksandr Solzhenitsyn (written 1958–68 and first published in 1973) eventually reached an international mass audience. In the United States, the Southern cradle during the era of Jim Crow spawned Martin Luther King Jr.'s *Letter from Birmingham Jail* (1963), Harper Lee's *To Kill a Mockingbird* (1960), ragtime, gospel, and jazz. The efforts to shut down the civil rights and the anti-war movements gave us the songs "We Shall Overcome," "Blowing in the Wind," and Lennon's "Give Peace a Chance." The attempt to oppose the artist has, historically, empowered the arts. But no artist wishes to be motivated and empowered in that way because they know that oppression destroys. This is why many successful artists did not rest on their laurels but became activists in the 1950s and 1960s.

To face the future of theatre, we have to look back at history. Theatre is a discipline that continually digs into the tradition while keeping an eye on innovation. Juggling the past and the present can result in magnificent discoveries. The direction that theatre takes will likely involve a continued examination of issues that dominate our attention today. Eventually, a voice or two might emerge as the definitive one for our epoch. We must be cautious about crowning works in our own time. Celebrate, yes; bestow genius on it? Maybe. Time will tell.

Shakespeare was not the only playwright of the Tudor period. In fact, for many, he was not even the favorite. From 1592 to 1596, his plays were performed outdoors at Richard Burbage's The Globe and Philip Henslowe's The Rose. After Burbage purchased Blackfriars in 1596 and made Shakespeare a partner, his plays were performed in both theatres. One of his plays, *As You Like It*, was performed at the Temple Inn Theatre. However, Queen Elizabeth's favorite play was Thomas Kyd's *The Spanish Tragedy* (1582–92), and her favorite playwright was Ben Jonson. Therefore, the question is: how many Ben Jonson or Thomas Kyd festivals are there? None. I have seen one Ben Jonson play, *The Alchemist* (1610), at

Open Space Theatre in Seattle. Interestingly, the play has two Ana-baptist characters who deliver strident sermons in a Puritan style. Today, only Shakespeare is widely produced from that era.

Theatre in the West began in 576 BCE in Athens, and even though there have been a few interruptions, this tradition has returned to its roots, developed, and remains vibrant in our age. The interruptions occurred in the early medieval era when ecclesiastical edicts prohibited the performance of theatricals. Theatricals of that time, 500 CE, were, at large, displays of violent exchanges and sexual content, so the ban may seem reasonable to many. Nude scenes and gladiator battles were typical. The Greek tragedies always had death happen offstage, but the Romans changed all that and brought it onstage![8] More gore, more gore! The original scripts by the Greeks were greatly revised by Seneca and others for Roman audiences.

Due to the ecclesiastical ban, Roman and Greek theatres remained empty from the fifth until the tenth centuries. Traveling companies performed farces in the marketplaces and inns. Inns often had a central courtyard featuring evening entertainment for travelers. Hamlet encounters one such troupe (2.3), who will later catch the conscience of the king. Minstrels also emerged as popular storytellers and entertainers.

However, oppression and exclusion did not hold the final hand, and eventually, the church invited performances back on Easter Sunday in 921 CE at St. Gall, Switzerland. The ecclesiastical authorities had banned theatre, but when they wanted to revitalize worship, they brought the theatre back![9] And from that decade onward, no political or religious institution has ever been successful again in squelching theatricals for any long period of time. The Puritans ruled for a scant eighteen years. The persistence of performance in the West indicates a deep level of dedication, innovation, and adaptation. No one, not even a psychic network, has ever been able to predict the works that will draw us into the theatre next year and the next. There appears to be an irresistible

8. Dodge, "Amusing the Masses." Also Futrell, *Blood in the Arena.*

9. Young, *Drama of the Medieval Church.*

hunger for what theatre is and does because it exists in every culture around the globe. The same is true for music, dance, and the visual and literary arts. The arts exist to surprise us because they are our best renewable resource! The medieval church is a great example of religion's need for a theatrical interpretation of the faith.

Global awareness, diversity, international dialogue, and, by way of contrast, a new regionalism may be the future of the arts and, thus, aesthetics. People have been on the move for millennia, and in the past, they often willingly or were forced to abandon their previous culture. But that is not the trend today. Branches of Christianity, Buddhism, Islam, Hinduism, Judaism, Jainism, Sikhism, First Nation, and other faith groups now carry their religions with them as they move to new countries. The United States shows diverse religious traditions, and for smaller communities, this is an encouraging development. These trends coincide with the growth of the arts. The arts are the most diverse of all methods of communication, and at the same time, there is considerable international transfer of genres. It might be ironic that as the United States increases in the number of its subcultures, it is possibly becoming more homogenous artistically. Music, theatre, visual arts, fashion, dance, and literature are moving rapidly toward a global culture with regional differences. This is a new cauldron in which global humanism is cooking up a storm! The arts often retain their regional identity as they welcome diversity. Awareness of our global context will ask us to integrate artistic regionalism and diversity as we develop the courage to aim the spotlight into the future. Contemplating future possibilities also means coming to terms with ultimate reality and our own fragility. And through it all, may you also find a slant of light that beckons you onward.

The arts are a reminder that ideals such as goodness, charity, and justice can inspire people to action, but they have limitations when they intersect with life's situations. When we shift from the concept of justice to creating restorative justice, ambiguities emerge. We know the familiar saying that giving people a fish feeds them that day, but teaching people how to fish will feed them for life. But who does that? Actualization of ethical ideals engages us in historical situations where ideals meet the rough stuff of human existence and ambiguity. As the Good Book states, "we now see through a glass darkly." Without knowing the outcome, we forge ahead with the ideals that motivate us. But to enact justice, restorative justice exposes us to ambiguity because we can seldom predict all the consequences of our actions. The arts are a continual reminder of our situation in history. We forge ahead without guarantees of success. A person goes into surgery, and the physician says, 99 percent of the time, this is successful. And the listening pessimist interprets this to mean that they are the one percent.

The arts, on the other hand, are vehicles of hope amid the existential crises of history and our personal lives. Just to know where a rift line exists informs the builder of the danger that lurks beneath the surface. When, where, and how we will react to those dangers is ambiguous, even when we are inspired by our ideals. Restorative justice is where ideals and existential realities intersect. Thus, that is where we will find the arts. There, we will forge an authentic life by making those connections. Art persists so that we might thrive.

Addendum

The publication of Heidegger's *Black Notebooks* (2014)[1] revealed the depth of his philosophical alignment with National Socialism. Prior to that publication, there were questions about his dedication to what became the German "dive" into the abyss. The faculty at the University of Freiburg elected him as rector (president) in 1934, and he reluctantly accepted their decision. His inaugural address outlined how he thought universities could provide a vision for a new Germany rooted in its national "character," which he assumed would provide a philosophical foundation for the National Socialist agenda. After nine months as rector, he resigned because his vision for the University was in direct conflict with demands from the Berlin regime. Philosophers George Steiner and Hannah Arendt were quick to point out that his rectorship was an error and that his resignation demonstrated his intellectual distance from the Nazi regime.[2] In addition, before the Wannsee Conference (the Nazi leadership conference at which Hitler's final solution was presented) in January 1942, Heidegger was dismissed from the University and assigned to an earthwork crew along the Rhine. His flirtation with the National Socialists was a brief episode and ended with his resignation from the rectorship. To many, including myself, that decision illustrated his resistance to the Nazi agenda. The dismissal was additional proof. But we had not read the *Black Notebooks*.

1. Heidegger, *Ponderings, I–XV: Black Notebooks*.
2. Steiner, *Martin Heidegger*, 121; Arendt, *Letters 1925–1975*, 237.

According to Richard Wolin,[3] the *Black Notebooks* reveal that Heidegger's philosophical commitments continued to be aligned with the National Socialist agenda for Germany: a national identity for Germans by Germans, including a primacy of German culture, race, and language. All others are benefactors, interlopers, or abusers of this agenda. Heidegger's intellectual framework did not advocate this point of view, but it allowed it to flourish, and he never opposed this (mis)reading of his ideas. It is now difficult to make the claim that his leaning toward National Socialism was a brief episode and that he sought to distance himself from those ideas.

Heidegger continues to cast a large shadow over aesthetic and literary criticism. Is he worthy of analysis even after we see his compromised legacy? That is the question scholars grapple with today and will continue to do so, I predict, for some decades. It is quite possible that if I had known the content of the *Black Notebooks* at the time this essay was written, I would have relied on other philosophers to explain the artistic trends in the twentieth century.

Many philosophers have held dubious political and cultural views. Most have been nationalistic or ethnocentric, with the belief that their culture, race, and regime have qualities that make them superior to others. Those beliefs have often led to catastrophic events, including the Holocaust. For some scholars, the Holocaust is a crime that surpasses and is incomparable with other evils.[4] But if it is incomparable with other evils, then it is also incomprehensible. As a result, silence is often the response for those who do not comprehend its horrors.[5] Silence in the aftermath of the Holocaust might imply trauma, complicity, incomprehension, or indifference. Heidegger appears to stand with the latter.[6] From that

3. Wolin, *Heidegger in Ruins*, 223.

4. Rozett, "The Unprecedented Nature of the Holocaust and Its Unique Features."

5. Steiner, *Language and Silence.*

6. I make this assumption because in his letter exchange with Hannah Arendt he never mentions the Holocaust or the National Socialist death camps.

perspective, philosophers in the post-Holocaust era who failed to condemn the Nazi regime seem to be tarnished more than those who had ethical lapses in prior epochs. That is why some consider Heidegger to be in a category by himself.[7]

The problem also centers on who is German and who is not. This debate has preoccupied some German academics. Beginning with the unification of Germany in 1871, one side promoted the view that anyone who resided within the boundary of the German nation was German. The prior view, and the one Heidegger subscribes to, is that German culture and language identify who is German. Thus, Germans in the international diaspora, e.g., from Milwaukee to Rostov, should be viewed as German *Volk*. The investigation into German language origins and their meaning for German identity becomes his primary quest. The problem is exacerbated when linguistic origins are racialized. Are Jews or Poles who are fluent in German and who live within the national boundaries actual Germans? Heidegger believed they were not. He seems to have drawn the line where the National Socialists did. In his view, a German is identified by language, national boundaries, and the idea of a master race.

Historical studies cannot change history, but they may prepare us for a more just and equal future. The tendency in the West to construct a philosophical system on the assumption of cultural, political, and religious superiority has now seen the catastrophic results of that belief. May this impel scholars to investigate other traditions with a heightened sense of equality and equanimity?

It might also be appropriate to name other respected German scholars and artists who were quiet during the Nazi era or opposed totalitarianism but were silent on the Holocaust and anti-Semitism. As an American, one can also identify many scholars and artists who were silent about slavery and later Jim Crow laws. Are we Americans in a position to assess the moral failures of other cultures?

Hannah Arendt, *Letters 1925–1975*, 162. The key phrase: "It is a matter of indifference."

7. Wolin, *Heidegger in Ruins*, 245.

Thus, to include Heidegger in an essay has many pitfalls. To exclude him is also complicated. Complicated because his analysis, key terms, and emphasis on existential presence are still part of the global discussion on aesthetics. Therefore, in this publication, I will offer my recent observations on Heidegger with plans for a future reassessment.

Works Cited

"Acts and Ordinances of the Interregnum, 1642–1660." *British History Online.* Accessed May 1, 2023. https://www.british-history.ac.uk/no-series/acts-ordinances-interregnum/.

Adams, Douglas G. *Transcendence with the Human Body in Art.* New York: Crossroad, 1991.

Aiken, George. *Uncle Tom's Cabin; or, Life among the Lowly. A Domestic Drama in Six Acts.* 1854. Rpt. Gloucester, UK: 2008. The first published edition is online: http://utc.iath.virginia.edu/onstage/scripts/aikenhp.html

Alexander, Michelle. *The New Jim Crow.* New York: New Press, 2020.

Aquinas, Thomas. "Beauty Is a Kind of Knowledge." In *Readings in the History of Aesthetics: An Open-Source Reader*, chap. 4. Ver. 0.11. Accessed May 2, 2023. https://philosophy.lander.edu/intro/artbook/x1797.htm.

Arendt, Hannah. *Letters 1925–1975: Arendt and Heidegger.* New York: Harcourt, 2003.

Aristotle. *The Nicomachean Ethics.* Translated by David Ross. Oxford: Oxford University Press, 1998.

———. *Poetics.* Translated by Gerald F. Else. Ann Arbor, MI: University of Michigan Press, 1973.

Arnott, Peter. *Theatre in Its Time: An Introduction.* Boston: Little, Brown and Company, 1981.

"Augustinian Platonism." *Encyclopedia Britannica.* Accessed April 25, 2023. https://www.britannica.com/topic/Platonism/Augustinian-Platonism.

"Banksy." *Encyclopedia Britannica.* Accessed April 25, 2023. https://www.britannica.com/biography/Banksy.

"Beecher Bible and Rifle Church." Atlas Obscura. https://www.atlasobscura.com/places/beecher-bible-and-rifle-church

Bevington, David, ed. *The Complete Works of Shakespeare.* 4th ed. New York: Longman, 1997.

Björk, Mårten, and Jayne Svenungsson, eds. *Heidegger's "Black Books" and the Future of Theology.* London: Palgrave, 2014.

Brown, William Wells. *William Wells Brown: Clotel & Other Writings.* Edited by Ezra Greenspan. New York: Library of America, 2014.

Works Cited

Caglioti, Giuseppe. "Art according to Albert Einstein." Springer Link, March 21, 2017. https://link.springer.com/article/10.1007/s40329-017-0155-7.

Chekhov, Anton. *Plays*. Translated by Elisaveta Fen. London: Penguin, 1954.

Cawthon, Daniel. "Eugene O'Neill: Progenitor of a New Religious Drama." *Theatre and Religion* 1 (1992) 21–30.

Cote, David. "Theatre Review: 'Hamilton.'" *Time Out New York*, August 6, 2015.

Danto, Arthur. *After the End of Art*. Princeton: Princeton University Press, 1988.

———. *The Transfiguration of the Commonplace*. Cambridge: Harvard University Press, 1997.

Delman, Edward. "How Lin-Manuel Miranda Shapes History." *Atlantic*, September 19, 2015. https://www.theatlantic.com/entertainment/archive/2015/09/lin-manuel-miranda-hamilton/408019/.

Dewey, John. *Art as Experience*. New York: Putnam's Sons, 1958.

Dickie, George. *Aesthetics: An Introduction*. Indianapolis: Pegasus, 1971.

Dodge, Hazel. "Amusing the Masses." In *Life, Death, and Entertainment in the Roman Empire*, edited by D. S. Potter and D. J. Mattingly, 205–53. Ann Arbor, MI: University of Michigan Press, 1999.

Eliot, T. S. *The Complete Poems and Plays*. New York: Harcourt, Brace & World, 1962.

Elwell, J. Sage. "Humanism in the Arts." In *Oxford Handbook on Humanism*, edited by A. H. Pinn, 389–408. Oxford: Oxford University Press, 2021.

"Eugene O'Neill: A Controversial Play." PBS American Experience. Accessed April 25, 2023. https://www.pbs.org/wgbh/americanexperience/features/oneill-controversial-play/.

FastHorse, Larissa. *The Thanksgiving Play*. New York: French, 2019.

Freebody, Kelley. *Critical Themes in Drama*. London: Routledge, 2021.

Friesen, Duane. *Artists, Citizens, Philosophers*. Scottdale, PA: Herald, 2000.

Friesen, Lauren, and Dennis R. Koehn, eds. *Anabaptist ReMix: Varieties of Cultural Engagement in North America*. New York: Peter Lang, 2022.

Fukuyama, Francis. *The End of History and the Last Man*. New York: Free, 1992.

Futrell, Alison. *Blood in the Arena*. Austin, TX: University of Texas Press, 1997.

"Georg Wilhelm Friedrich Hegel." *Stanford Encyclopedia of Philosophy*. Accessed April 22, 2023. https://plato.stanford.edu/entries/hegel/.

Greene, Maxine. *Variations on a Blue Guitar: The Lincoln Center Institute Lectures on Aesthetic Education*. New York: Teachers College, 2001.

Hall, Edward. "Tell Your Story, Omar." *New York Review of Books*, April 25, 2023, 39–41.

Hamilton, Ruth. "Derek Jacobi—Claudius Contemplates Hamlet." *New York Times*, June 10, 1979, https://www.nytimes.com/1979/06/10/archives/derek-jacobiclaudius-contemplates-hamlet-derek-jacobi.html.

Harrington, Austin. *Art and Social Theory*. Cambridge: Polity, 2004.

Hegel, G. W. F. *The Philosophy of Fine Art*, vols. 1–4. Translated by F. P. B. Osmaston. London: Bell and Sons, 1920.

Works Cited

Heidegger, Martin. *Heidegger, Ponderings, I–XV: Black Notebooks*. Translated by Richard Rojcewicz. Bloomington, IN: Indiana University. 2014–17.

———. *Poetry, Language, and Thought*. Translated by Albert Hofstadter. New York: Harper & Row, 1975.

"Hilary A. Armstrong." *Encyclopedia Britannica*. Accessed April 25, 2023. https://www.britannica.com/topic/Platonism/Augustinian-Platonism.

Huizinga, Johan. *Homo Ludens*. 1938. Reprint, Mansfield Center, CT: Martino, 2014.

Kant, Immanuel. *Critique of Judgment*. Translated by J. H. Bernard. New York: Hafner, 1951.

Kenner, Hugh. "Life in the Box." In *Casebook on Waiting for Godot*, edited by Ruby Cohn, 107–13. New York: Grove, 1967.

Krasner, David. "Empathy and Theatre." In *Staging Philosophy*, edited by David Krasner and David Z. Saltz, 255–77. Ann Arbor, MI: University of Michigan, 2006.

Langer, Susanna K. *Feeling and Form*. New York: Scribner's Sons, 1953.

———. *Philosophy in a New Key*. Cambridge: Harvard University Press, 1978.

———. *Problems of Art*. New York: Scribner's Sons, 1957.

Marx, Karl. *Critique of the Gotha Program*. 1875. Translated by Kevin B. Anderson and Karel Ludenhoff, introduction by Peter Hudis, foreword by Peter Linebaugh. Oakland, CA: PM Press/Spectre, 2023. Accessed June 4, 2024. https://www.marxists.org/archive/marx/works/1875/gotha/ch01.htm.

McClendon, Jr., James Wm. *Ethics*. Nashville: Abingdon, 1986.

Miller, Arthur. *Playing for Time*. Downers Grove, IL: Dramatic, 1985.

Mousley, Andy. *Re-Humanizing Shakespeare*. Edinburgh: Edinburgh University Press, 2009.

Niebuhr, H. Richard. *Christ and Culture*. New York: Harper and Row, 1957.

Nietzsche, Friedrich W. *The Birth of Tragedy*. Edited by Raymond Geuss and Ronald Speirs. Cambridge: Cambridge University Press, 1999.

———. *Thus Spake Zarathustra*, https://www.gutenberg.org/files/1998/1998-h/1998-h.htm, LX, Fourth Part.

O'Neill, Eugene. "Eugene O'Neill: A Controversial Play." *American Experience*. PBS. Accessed April 25, 2023, https://www.pbs.org/wgbh/americanexperience/features/oneill-controversial-play/.

———. *The Plays of Eugene O'Neill*, Vol. 2. New York: Modern Library, 1982.

Online Books by William D'Avenant (D'Avenant, William, 1606–1668), accessed January 4, 2024, https://onlinebooks.library.upenn.edu/webbin/book/lookupname?key=D%27Avenant%2C%20William%2C%201606%2D1668.

Orkin, Martin. "Othello and the 'Plain Face' of Racism." *Shakespeare Quarterly* 38.2 (1987) 166–88.

Parks, Suzan-Lori. *Plays for the Plague Year*. New York: Theatre Communications Group, 2023.

Works Cited

Phillips, Maya, "Review: In 'Plays for the Plague Year,' the Soundtrack of Our Lives." *New York Times*, April 18, 2023. https://www.nytimes.com/2023/04/18/theater/plays-for-the-plague-year-review.html.

Plato. *Laws*. Edited by Malcolm Schofield. Cambridge: Cambridge University Press, 2016.

———. *Republic*. Translated by B. Jowett. New York: Vintage, 1956.

Powers, Anna. "Why Art Is Vital to the Study of Science." *Forbes*, July 31, 2020. Accessed May 4, 2023. https://www.forbes.com/sites/annapowers/2020/07/31/why-art-is-vital-to-the-study-of-science/?sh=305d3ed542eb.

Rawls, John. *A Theory of Justice*. Cambridge: Harvard University Press, 1971.

Redmond, James. *Themes in Drama*. 8 vols. Cambridge: Cambridge University Press, 1979–86.

Rockmore, Tom. *On Heidegger's Nazism and Philosophy*. Berkeley: University of California Press, 1991.

Rood, Wayne. *Theatre and Theology*. Berkeley, CA: C.A.R.E., 2000.

"Rosalind Franklin." Encyclopedia Britannica. Accessed April 20, 2023. https://www.britannica.com/topic/Platonism/Augustinian-Platonism.

Rothko, Mark. *The Artist's Reality*. Edited by Christopher Rothko. New Haven, CT: Yale University Press, 2004.

———. *Writings on Art*. Edited by Miguel Lopez-Remiro. New Haven, CT: Yale University Press, 2006.

Rozett, Robert. "The Unprecedented Nature of the Holocaust and Its Unique Features: Some Reflections—Part I." Accessed January 3, 2024. https://www.yadvashem.org/blog/the-unprecedented-nature-of-the-holocaust.html.

Sevier, Christopher. *Aquinas on Beauty*. New York: Lexington, 2015.

Shakespeare, William. *Othello*. Edited by David Bevington. New York: Simon and Schuster, 1993.

———. *Twelfth Night*. Edited by David Bevington. New York: Penguin, 1965.

Shaver-Gleason, Linda. "You Don't Need Science to Tell You Why You Like a Song." *The Outline* (blog) January 11, 2017. https://theoutline.com/post/876/you-dont-need-science-to-tell-you-why-you-like-a-song.

Shaw, Helen. "On Broadway." *New Yorker*, May 8, 2023, 7.

Sluga, Hans. *Heidegger's Crises: Philosophy and Politics in Nazi Germany*. Cambridge: Harvard University Press, 1995.

Soyinka, Wole. *Art, Dialogue, & Outrage*. Ibadan, Nigeria: New Horn, 1988.

———. *Death and the King's Horseman*. New York: Norton, 2002.

Steiner, George. *Language and Silence*. New Haven, CT: Yale University, 2013.

———. *Martin Heidegger*. New York: Viking, 1997.

Stowe, Harriet Beecher. *Uncle Tom's Cabin*. New Dehli: Sharp Ink, 2023. Amazon Kindle.

"Theodore Parker." Wikipedia. Accessed April 25, 2023. https://en.wikipedia.org/wiki/Theodore_Parker.

Works Cited

Thomas, Dylan. "The Force That through the Green Fuse Drives the Flower." Poetry.org. Accessed April 30, 2023. https://poets.org/poem/force-through-green-fuse-drives-flower.

Tillich, Paul. *On Art and Architecture*. Edited by John Dillenberger. New York: Crossroad, 1987.

———. *Systematic Theology*. Vol. 2. Chicago: University of Chicago Press, 1951.

Tsioulcas, Anastasia. "The Debut of 'Omar,' a Thoroughly American Opera." NPR, Morning Edition, June 7, 2022.

"William Davenant." Wikipedia. Accessed January 4, 2024. https://en.wikipedia.org/wiki/William_Davenant.

Williams, Takim, "#InContext: Cornel West." The Human Trafficking Institute, February 22, 2017, https://traffickinginstitute.org/incontext-cornel-west/#:~:text=%E2%80%9CJustice%20is%20what%20love%20looks%20like%20in%20public%2C,Theological%20Seminary%20and%20Professor%20Emeritus%20at%20Princeton%20University.

Wolin, Richard. *Heidegger in Ruins: Between Philosophy and Ideology*. New Haven, CT: Yale University Press, 2023.

Index

Index

beauty, 16–18, 45, 46, 49, 60–61, 91
Beckett, Samuel, 54–55
Beecher family, 68
beingness. *See* existence/beingness
Bible, 49, 51, 57, 93, 97
Black Notebooks (Heidegger), 99–100
Brecht, Bertolt, 92
Brown, William Wells, 67, 69

catharsis
  Aristotle on, 14, 15, 77
  community and, 91–92
  Danto on, 52–53
  justice and, 71, 73, 77–78, 79–80, 81, 85–86
  Langer on, 33–34, 35
  preservation as, 89
cathedrals, 17
chaos, 29, 63, 66, 70, 71, 85
Chekhov, Anton, 37
Christianity, 10, 16–18, 93–94, 95
  See also Bible; God; Jesus; theology
Christo, 57, 58–59
civil rights movement, 15, 24, 94
clarity, 17, 43
climactic moments, 14–15
colonialism, 70–72, 78–80
colors, 17
community, 58, 59, 62, 63, 89–93
  See also society
cooking, 8
COVID-19, 88–89
cultures
  diversity of, 26–27, 79, 85, 96
  superiority assumptions in, 2, 27, 100
  understanding across, 61–62, 70–71, 72, 79, 82

Danto, Arthur, 31–32, 50–56, 81, 84, 86–87
D'Avenant, William, 10–11, 93–94

decoration, 46
democracy, 61, 63
desire, 27
deus ex machina, 14, 29
Dewey, John, 31, 36–39
dialect, 74
dialectic, 23–26
Dickie, George, 31, 47–50
disclosure
  aesthetic experiences and, 62
  end of art and, 53
  Heidegger on, 42–47
  material and, 45–46, 55
  See also truth
discovery, 60, 62, 63
discursive expression, 32, 34
diversity/multiplicity
  Aristotle on, 13
  of character interpretations, 48–49
  of cultures, 26–27, 79, 85, 96
  of responses to art, 5–6, 20–23, 46–47
drama. *See* theatre
durability, 21, 49, 68, 83
duty, 10, 13, 78

economic justice, 87, 92
education, 60, 62, 63
Einstein, Albert, 5
El Fin del Mundo (Valdez), 88
emotions
  in aesthetic experiences, 6, 15, 19, 34, 39, 62
  Aristotle on, 14–15
  Augustine on, 16
  awareness of, 34, 35, 60, 86
  community and, 91–92
  Danto on, 52–53
  Dewey on, 36, 39
  Greene on, 60, 61, 62
  Hegel on, 27
  Heidegger on, 46–47
  Kant on, 19
  Langer on, 32–34, 35

Index

Rockmore, Tom, 41
Romans, 95
Romantics, 45, 87
Roosevelt, F. D., 15
Rothko, Mark, 8, 22, 34, 57
Running Fence (Christo), 58–59

Schwartz, Stephen, 92
science, 4–5, 15, 21, 22
scientific rationalism, 45
sculptures, 52, 53, 57–58
Segal, George, 57
sensation, 18
Shakespeare, William, 11, 22, 27,
    48–49, 75–78, 94
Shanley, John Patrick, 92
slavery, 67–70, 82–83
Sluga, Hans, 41
society
    catharsis and, 14, 15
    changes in, 70
    Greene on, 61, 62, 63
    in Hegelian dialectic, 26, 28
    justice and, 65–66, 72–74,
        79–80, 81, 83, 85–86, 87,
        92–93
    in Plato's idealism, 9
    See also community
Solzhenitsyn, Aleksandr, 94
Sophocles, 13, 14–15, 24–25, 54
Soviet Union, 28, 94
Soyinka, Wole, 31, 49, 70–72
spectacle, 13–14
spirit, 24, 25–26, 27, 28, 29, 68
stained glass, 17
Steiner, George, 40, 99
Stowe, Harriet Beecher, 67–70
structure, 32, 33, 35
subjectivity, 18–19, 20–23
the sublime, 19
subtext, 71–72
suicide, 71, 92
synthesis, 23–26, 29, 33–34, 53,
    84–85

talent, 27
Terry, Megan, 21
Thanksgiving Play, The (Fast-
    Horse), 78–80
theatre
    Aristotle on, 12–15, 54
    colonialism in, 70–72, 78–80
    community and, 89–93
    end of art and, 81–82, 87–89,
        92–93
    future of, 93, 95–97
    in institutional theory, 48–49
    interracial relationships in,
        72–74, 75–78
    justice investigated in, 64–67
    origins of, 95
    Plato on, 8–9, 10, 11
    religion and, 10–11, 82, 92,
        93–94, 95
    slavery in, 67–70, 82–83
    themes, 64–65, 70, 71–72, 87,
        92–93
theology, 16–18
    See also Bible; Christianity;
        God; Jesus; religion
Thomas, Aquinas, Saint, 16–18, 43
Thomas, Dylan, 16
thought, 18, 32–34, 35
Tillich, Paul, 59–60, 75
Tolstoy, Leo, 26, 28
tragedies, 11, 14
transcendence, 59
transfiguration/transformation
    in art, 51–52, 55, 81
    of audiences, 39, 44, 52, 55, 59,
        61, 91–92
truth, 8, 20, 44–47, 56, 57, 74
    See also disclosure
Two Trains Running (Wilson), 88

Uncle Tom's Cabin (Stowe), 67–70
unity, 9, 58
unstructured emotions, 35

Valdez, Luis, 88